SELECTED US FLAGS 1775–76

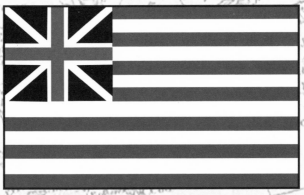

GRAND UNION FLAG ~ THE FIRST NATIONAL FLAG INCORPORATED
THE UNION JACK; CARRIED BY THE REVOLUTIONARY FORCES.

GADSDEN FLAG ~ FLOWN BY THE CONTINENTAL NAVY, 1775;
THE RATTLESNAKE FLAG BECAME A LIBERTARIAN SYMBOL.

BETSY ROSS FLAG ~ LEGEND HAS IT THAT THE PHILADELPHIA
SEAMSTRESS BASED THIS FLAG ON WASHINGTON'S DESIGN, 1776.

THE POCKET BOOK OF PATRIOTISM

by Jonathan Foreman

STERLING PUBLISHING
New York

Published by Sterling Publishing Co., Inc.
387 Park Avenue South, New York, NY 10016

© 2005 by Halstead Books, Ltd.

Distributed in Canada by Sterling Publishing
c/o Canadian Manda Group, 165 Dufferin Street
Toronto, Ontario M6K 3H6

ISBN: 1-4027-2990-1

Library of Congress Cataloging-in-Publication Data
Foreman, Jonathan.
    The pocket book of patriotism / Jonathan Foreman.
    p. cm.
    ISBN 1-4027-2990-1 (alk. paper)
    1. Patriotism--United States--Miscellanea.   I. Title.
JK1759.F65 2005
323.6'5--dc22

                                            2005014628

1 3 5 7 9 8 6 4 2

Map on endpapers: Details from a 1797 engraving of America showing the original 13 colonies and the largely unexplored West

Printed and bound in the United States of America

For information about custom editions, special sales, premium and corporate purchases, please contact Sterling Special Sales Department at 800-805-5489 or specialsales@sterlingpub.com.

CONTENTS

INTRODUCTION   5

PART ONE
TIMELINE OF AMERICAN & WORLD HISTORY   7

PART TWO
PATRIOTIC TEXTS & ESSENTIALS   65
(ALL TEXTS EXCERPTS EXCEPT WHERE NOTED)

- Speeches, Charters & Significant Documents 66
- Songs 79
- Poems & Verse 86
- United States Presidents 88
- The States in Order of Joining the Union 89
- What Is Patriotism? (Quotations) 90
- Medals for Valor 92
- Flag Tradition & Etiquette 94
- Oaths & Pledges 96

*With thanks to the men and women of the 54th Engineer Battalion
and the 4th Battalion/64th Armored Regiment, US Army,
and to Justine.*

INTRODUCTION

The Pocket Book of Patriotism is a primer intended to fill some of the void left by the abandonment of traditional civic instruction in America.

It is not a textbook, still less an encyclopedia. It is a celebration of this country. Without whitewashing America's past (true patriotism acknowledges America's sins and flaws) it celebrates America's history, her contributions to humanity, the eternal optimism and energy of her people. Above all it celebrates the documents in which successive generations of Americans have placed their faith.

It begins with a timeline because chronology has been one of the casualties of certain modern educational trends and because it's impossible to understand or appreciate history without knowing the order of events.

Not long ago a friend told me how a clever teenage girl of her acquaintance, a student at a top Manhattan private school, wasn't sure which came first: the Vietnam War or the Italian Renaissance. There is something very wrong when even the most expensive American education leaves children adrift and confused about which things happened when, in their own country and the rest of the world.

The timeline is a selective, not a comprehensive one. It includes some landmarks that may have received too little attention in recent histories; it also reflects the author's view that while America's record is stained by the original sin of slavery and by many episodes of cruelty, intolerance, and fraternal struggle, Americans have much more of which to be proud than ashamed. Our history is tragic in parts, but it is overwhelmingly a glorious and inspiring one. The Abroad column of the timeline is intended to put key events in our history in a global chronological context.

The second section of the book features speeches, quotations, and songs that inspired generations of American children but which have largely disappeared from our schools and our popular culture. Also featured are highlights from the great documents—including the Declaration of Independence and the Constitution—that embody America's founding ideals, and which have inspired her heroes from 1776 to today.

It may be useful at this point to say what patriotism is and is not. Patriotism is not the same as nationalism; it has nothing to do with xenophobia. As Adlai Stevenson wrote, "Men who have offered their lives for their country know that patriotism is not the fear of something, it is the love of something." The most impressive patriots that I have met are men and women wearing their country's uniform who are clearly inspired by love of country and love of its ideals. It may even be that love of your own country and countrymen is a prerequisite to genuine affection for foreign people and places.

Perhaps the most important idea underlying this book is that American patriotism is different than other patriotisms in the same way that the United States is different from other countries. Unlike foreign patriotisms, American patriotism has almost nothing to do with notions of blood and soil. We, alone, are a people dedicated to a proposition. American patriotism has everything to do with the political ideas that inspired the founders, and which found expression in living documents that continue to shape the destiny of the United States. American patriotism also has a great deal to do with faith in human possibility, that belief in a better future that inspired successive waves of colonists and immigrants.

The United States was blessed by providence in the education and character of its founding generation: leaders steeped in the best of England's Whiggish traditions and common law, classical learning, and the thoughtful questioning prompted by the European Enlightenment. The documents they drew up are a defining element of American life in a way that the written constitutions of other countries are generally not.

It is because of those documents and their extraordinary role in our culture that American patriotism is inclusive. It is generous. It tolerates dissent. Sometimes it even mandates dissent, because American patriotism cannot be separated from America's ideals. The fact that these ideals have too often been honored in the breach, even at our country's moment of birth, means that no American should confuse America's good fortune with perfection.

But for all that American patriotism acknowledges the nation's faults and for all that it celebrates diversity of opinion and ethnic origin, it also implies duties and responsibilities. You are not a patriot if you betray the trust of your fellow citizens. That is a lesson I learned from my father, the screenwriter Carl Foreman. Though he was an American driven into exile by the infamous Hollywood blacklist, he remained an American citizen and a proud one. I remember his horror and disgust as a patriot and former GI at the spectacle of an American actress who posed with enemy soldiers in wartime.

Patriotism comes in many forms, small and large. (As Adlai Stevenson also said, it is "not a short and frenzied outburst of emotion but the tranquil and steady dedication of a lifetime.") And you can find it in every walk of life. But for me personally, the touchstone of patriotism is represented by the men and women I met as an embedded reporter with the US Army during Operation Iraqi Freedom. They were my inspiration as I compiled the *Pocket Book of Patriotism*. Accordingly, it is dedicated to them.

PART ONE

Timeline of American & World History

THE AMERICAS	ABROAD
30,000–20,000 BC Bering Strait crossed by ancestors of American Indians **11,000–9000 BC** Ice recedes, breaking Bering land bridge	
	c 10,000 BC First settled agriculture, animal domestication, bow and arrow **c 3500 BC** First cities built on Fertile Crescent **c 3300 BC** Earliest writing on Sumerian clay tablets **c 3100–1500 BC** Stonehenge circle **c 3100 BC** Egypt united; invention of hieroglyphic writing
3000–1800 BC Norte Chico civilization, coastal Peru	**c 2700 BC** Agriculture reaches China **c 2600–1700 BC** Indus Valley urban civilization in Northern India **c 2550 BC** Great Pyramid of Khufu, Egypt
c 2000 BC Inuit culture, Southwest Alaska and Aleutian Islands	**c 1890 BC** Babylon founded **c 1700 BC** "Eye for an Eye" Code of Hammurabi becomes law in Babylon **c 1600–1046 BC** Shang Dynasty in China, first Chinese writing **c 1500–900 BC** Hindu *Vedas* composed
	1333–1323 BC Tutankhamen, pharoah of Egypt **c 1250 BC** Trojan War **c 1225 BC** Moses presents Ten Commandments to Israelites
1200–800 BC Olmec civilization, Mexico's Gulf Coast	**c 1200 BC** Beginning of Iron Age **c 1000 BC** David, King of Israel **c 900 BC** Homer's *Iliad*, *Odyssey* **776 BC** First Olympic Games, Greece
c 700 BC Zapotecs build city of Monte Albán, Central Mexico	**604 BC** Birth of Lao-Tzu, founder of Taoism **563 BC** Buddha born in India **510 BC** Roman Republic founded **508 BC** Democratic reforms in Athens, Golden Age begins **490 BC** Athenian victory over Persians at Marathon

480 BC Battle of Salamis, Greek fleet defeats Xerxes' Persians
479 BC Death of Confucius

431–404 BC Athens fights Sparta in Peloponnesian War
399 BC Trial and death of Socrates
384–322 BC Life of Aristotle
c 380 BC Plato's *The Republic*
334–323 BC Alexander the Great conquers empire from Greece to India

c 273 BC Ashoka, emperor of India
221 BC China unified by Ch'in dynasty; construction of Great Wall
218 BC Hannibal of Carthage crosses Alps to attack Rome
206 BC–AD 220 Han Dynasty, China
146 BC Rome destroys Carthage, subordinates Greece

73–71 BC Spartacus slave revolt, Rome
58–50 BC Julius Caesar conquers Gaul; flowering of Latin literature
44 BC Julius Caesar murdered
31 BC Augustus, first Roman emperor
30 BC Mark Antony, Cleopatra of Egypt commit suicide
c 3 BC Birth of Jesus
AD 30 Jesus crucified
AD 37–41 Caligula, Roman Emperor
AD 43 Rome conquers Celtic Britain
c AD 50 London founded
AD 70 Romans sack Jerusalem, destroy Temple
AD 79 Vesuvius erupts, destroys Pompeii

c AD 100 Pyramid of Sun built at Teotihuacan, Mexico
c AD 100 Tiahuanaco civilization near Lake Titicaca, Peru
c 100–400 Hopewell culture, moundbuilding civilization in Northeast and Midwest

c 200–800 Nazca lines created, Peru
c 200–900 Mayan city-states dominate
Central America

293 Roman Empire split between two
emperors, East and West
c 300 Invention of stirrup
320–540 Gupta dynasty in India
330 Emperor Constantine founds
Constantinople at Byzantium

c 400–500 Yamato Kings unite Japan
c 400 Rise of Christian Kingdom of
Axium (Ethiopia)
409 Roman Legions abandon Britain
c 410 St. Augustine's *City of God*
450–750 Dark Ages in Britain; England
settled by Angles, Saxons, Jutes
453 Death of Attila the Hun, "Scourge
of God"
476 Last Western Roman Emperor
overthrown, fall of Rome to Visigoths

532 Buddhism introduced to Japan
534 Law Code of Justinian
537 Hagia Sophia Cathedral of
Constantinople completed

c 600 Mayans build sacred city of
Chichén Itzá, Mexico

c 600 Bamiyan Buddhas built,
Afghanistan
619–906 Tang Dynasty, China
625 Mohammed begins to recite Koran
632 Death of Mohammed, Sunni-Shia
split divides Islamic world
640 Arabs begin conquest of Middle
East, Central Asia, Mediterranean

c 700 Teotihuacan sacked and burned
by Toltecs

c 700–800 Gunpowder invented, China
c 700–1100 Global warming dries up
Silk Route wells
700–1911 Arabs import slaves from
East Africa
711 Arabs conquer Spain
732 Charles Martel defeats Arabs at
Tours, France
c 750 *Beowulf* saga composed

The Americas	Abroad
	751 Buddhist Diamond Sutra—first known printed book
	751 Charlemagne becomes Holy Roman (German) Emperor
	788 Work begins on Great Mosque at Cordoba, Spain
	866 Viking invasions of Britain
	889 Angkor temple complex founded, Cambodia
c 900 Great Mayan cities abandoned	
900–1350 Mississippi mound-builders	
1000 Viking Leif Eriksson explores Vinland (Newfoundland)	**c 1000–1200** Romany Gypsies leave India for Europe
	1054 East-West schism of Church
	1066 Norman Conquest of England
	1071 Seljuk Turks take Jerusalem
	1094 El Cid takes Valencia
	1096–99 First Crusade retakes Jerusalem from Muslims
	1118 Knights Templar established
	1119 Bologna University, first in Europe
1125 Aztecs arrive in Valley of Mexico	**1140** West adopts Arabic numerals
	1163 Work begins on Notre Dame, Paris
	1167 Oxford University founded
	1174 Leaning Tower of Pisa built
	1187 Saladin defeats Crusader Kingdom, captures Jerusalem
	1190 Richard the Lionheart leads Third Crusade, fails to capture Jerusalem
	1204 Constantinople, Greek Orthodox capital, sacked by Fourth Crusade
	1206–27 Genghis Khan's Mongol "Golden Horde" begins Asian conquest
	1209 Cambridge University founded
	1210–16 Dominican and Franciscan Orders founded
	1215 Magna Carta forced on King John I of England
	1238 Mongols take Moscow
	1260 Kublai Khan becomes Mongol Emperor, founds Yuan dynasty, China

	1271 Marco Polo leaves for China
	1281–1922 Ottoman Empire, Turkey
	1290 Jews expelled from England

c 1300–1400 Anasazi pueblos in American Southwest abandoned amidst war and cannibalism

c 1325 Aztecs build Tenochtitlan, begin conquest of Mexico basin

c 1300 Gunpowder reaches West, Arabs invent first gun
1307 Dante's *Divine Comedy*
1308 Papacy moved from Rome to Avignon
1327 Ibn Battuta begins travels across Asia and Africa
1337 Hundred Years War begins with English invasion of France
1347–50 Black Death plague kills third of Europe's population
1350–1850 Little Ice Age
1387 Chaucer's *Canterbury Tales*

c 1400 Renaissance begins in Italy
1405–33 Chinese fleet visits Africa, Persian Gulf, Southeast Asia

1415 Henry V's archers defeat French cavalry at Agincourt
1430 Joan of Arc burnt at stake
1434 Portuguese bring first slaves from Africa to Europe

1438 Inca Empire established from Ecuador to Chile
1450 Iroquois Confederacy formed

1450 Gutenberg Bible, first printed book in Europe
1453 Fall of Constantinople to Ottoman Turks drives European exploration
1478 Spanish Inquisition established

1458 Aztec empire extends through Mexico and Guatemala
1487 Aztecs sacrifice and eat 14,000 prisoners to dedicate Great Pyramid at Tenochtitlan

1488 Bartolomeu Dias rounds Cape of Good Hope

The Age of Discovery

1492 Christopher Columbus reaches Bahamas, Cuba, and Hispaniola:

1492 Spain unified under Ferdinand and Isabella; Moors and Jews expelled

"West, nothing to the north, nothing to the south."
COLUMBUS'S COURSE FROM CANARY ISLANDS

1493 Papal bull divides New World between Spain and Portugal
1493–96 Columbus's second voyage to Caribbean establishes colony in Santo Domingo, Hispaniola
1497 John Cabot, sailing for England, explores North American coastline, claims land for Henry VII
1498–1500 Columbus's third voyage: reaches Trinidad, Venezuela; arrested and sent home in shackles
1499 Amerigo Vespucci, sailing for Spain, discovers mouth of Amazon
1502–4 Columbus's fourth and final voyage
1507 New World referred to as "America" by German mapmaker

1494 Fall of Medicis, Florence

1497 Vasco da Gama finds passage to India around Africa

1503 Leonardo da Vinci's *Mona Lisa*
1507 Death of Cesare Borgia
1508 Michelangelo begins work on Sistine Chapel, Rome
1509 Henry VIII ascends throne of England

1510 First African slaves brought to Spanish New World
1511 Hernán Cortés and Diego Velasquez conquer Cuba
1513 Balboa crosses Panama, sees Pacific
1513 Ponce de León, searching for fountain of youth, reaches Florida

1510–1961 Portuguese occupy Goa

1511–13 Portuguese reach Molucca Spice Islands
1513 Machiavelli's *The Prince*

1514 Copernicus theorizes that the Earth circles the Sun
1516 Thomas More's *Utopia*
1516–1866 Jewish Ghetto, Venice
1517 Martin Luther's 95 Theses nailed to door of Wittenberg Cathedral

1519 Cortés lands in Yucatan, Mexico, with 500 men

	1520 Suleiman the Magnificent becomes Ottoman Emperor
	1520–21 Magellan's fleet
1521 Cortés captures Tenochtitlan with help of Indian allies; Aztec emperor Montezuma II killed:	circumnavigates the globe

"What men in the world have shown such daring?"
BERNAL DÍAZ DEL CASTILLO, CONQUISTADOR

	1521 Edict of Worms forbids Lutheran teachings; Protestant Reformation begins
1524 Verrazano explores New York Harbor; killed in 1528 by natives	**1526** Bābur founds Mughal Empire in India
	1529 Ottoman Turks take Budapest, attack Vienna
1532–3 Pizarro lands in Peru; captures Inca capital, executes Atahualpa	
1532 Cortés conquers all of Mexico	
	1533 Henry VIII of England excommunicated by Pope
1534 Jacques Cartier begins his exploration of Cananda	**1534–1917** Ottoman Turks occupy Mesopotamia (Iraq)
	1534 Ignatius Loyola founds Jesuit order, Rome
	1534 Church of England breaks with Rome
1535 Viceroyalty of New Spain established in Mexico	**1536** Protestant reformer John Calvin invited to Geneva
1536 Buenos Aires founded	**1536** Henry VIII executes second wife Anne Boleyn for adultery; marries Jane Seymour
	1536 Counter-Reformation begins
1539–42 Hernando de Soto lands in Florida; explores Gulf, Mississippi River Valley	**1539** Death of Guru Nanak, founder of Sikhism
1540–42 Coronado explores Southwest	
	1541 John Knox leads Calvinist Reformation in Scotland

1542 Bishop Bartolomé de las Casas, former conquistador, reports to Spanish crown "on the destruction of the Indies":

"Great atrocities are committed against the indigenous people."

1543 Firearms brought to Japan by shipwrecked Portuguese sailors

1546 Spanish crush last Mayan holdouts in Yucatan, Mexico

1547 Russia's Ivan the Terrible adopts title of "Tsar"
1549 Francis Xavier brings Christianity to Japan

1551 Universities founded in Mexico City and Lima, first in Western Hemisphere
1555–67 French found colony in Rio de Janeiro; defeated and expelled by Portuguese

1556–1605 Akbar the Great, mogul ruler of India
1558 English lose Calais, last possession in France
1558 Elizabeth I becomes Queen of England
1564 Birth of Shakespeare

1565 Spain establishes St. Augustine, Florida, first European settlement in North America

1566 Protestant Holland rebels against Spanish rule
1571 Don John of Austria smashes Ottoman fleet at Lepanto

1572 Spanish crush last Inca holdout in Peru; Tupac Amaru beheaded

1572 St. Bartholomew's Day Massacre, Paris: 20,000 Protestants slaughtered
1574–1604 Sikhs build Golden Temple at Amritsar
1575 Michel de Montaigne's *Essays*

1579 Frances Drake claims California for England as "Nova Albion"
1580–1640 Horses introduced to American Southwest by Spanish
1585 Roanoke Island colony organized by Sir Walter Raleigh
1586 Drake razes St. Augustine, Cartagena, Santo Domingo colonies

1582–98 Hideyoshi unites Japan, attacks Korea and China

1586 Colonists introduce potatoes and tobacco to England

AMERICA	ABROAD
1587 Virginia Dare, first child in America born to English parents, Roanoke	**1587** Drake raid on Cádiz, home port of Spanish Navy
	1587 Mary Queen of Scots executed
	1588 Spanish Armada invasion fleet defeated by English
c 1589 Unexplained disappearance of Roanoke Colony	**1589–1600** Richard Hakluyt's *Voyages* boosts curiosity about New World
	1594 Shakespeare's *Romeo and Juliet*
	1598 Edict of Nantes gives French Protestants freedom to worship
	1600 Shakespeare's *Hamlet* performed
	1603 Tokugawa clan wins Shogunate in Japan; restricts foreign trade
	1605–15 Miguel de Cervantes's *Don Quixote*
	1606 Italians obtain secret of chocolate, break Spanish monopoly

Founding a City on a Hill

1607 Virginia Company founds Jamestown colony with 120 colonists:

"Let England knowe our willingnesse,/For that our worke is good,/
We hope to plant a nation/Where none before hath stood."
NEWES FROM VIRGINIA 1610

AMERICA	ABROAD
1607 Jamestown leader John Smith captured by Powhatans, rescued by Pocahontas	
1608 Quebec, first French settlement of North America, founded by Samuel Champlain	**1608** First East India company vessels land in Surat, India
1609 Henry Hudson explores Northeast, Hudson River	
1609–10 "Starving Time" in Jamestown	
1610 Gov. Thomas Gates imposes harsh martial law on Jamestown	
1610 Spanish establish Santa Fe	
	1611 King James Bible
1614 Dutch found Ft. Nassau (Albany)	

1614–16 Epidemic decimates Indian tribes of New England

1616 Blue Mosque completed, Constantinople
1618–48 Thirty Years War devastates Germany

1619 Democracy comes to New World with Jamestown's "House of Burgesses"
1619 Dutch traders bring first African slaves to Virginia
1620 Mayflower Compact
1620 First Pilgrim expedition arrives at New Plymouth
1621 Puritans survive winter thanks to Patuxet tribesman Squanto; first Thanksgiving
1622 Jamestown settlers massacred in surprise Indian attack
1623 Second expedition of English settlers, Cape Ann

1619 English East India Company sets up first outpost in India at Surat

1624 Cardinal Richelieu takes effective power in France

1625 Dutch buy Manhattan for sixty guilders; found New Amsterdam

1625 French Protestants (Huguenots) revolt against Catholic rule
1626 St. Peter's Cathedral consecrated in Rome
1628 William Harvey discovers circulation of blood
1629 Charles I dissolves English Parliament

c 1630–1700 Beaver Wars begin: Dutch-armed Iroquois fight French and Algonquins
1630 First great Pilgrim fleet arrives
1630 John Winthrop, governor of Massachusetts Bay Company:

"We must consider that we shall be as a city upon a hill.
The eyes of all people are upon us."

1632 Death of Sweden's Gustavus Adolphus, "Lion of the North"
1633 Inquisition forces Galileo to recant belief in the Earth revolving the Sun

1634 Lord Baltimore founds Maryland, open to Catholic settlement

AMERICA	ABROAD
1635 Roger Williams expelled from Massachusetts, founds Rhode Island	
1636 Harvard College founded, first institution of higher learning in North America	**1636** Manchus take Beijing, establish Ching Dynasty
1636 Puritan leader Thomas Hooker founds Hartford colony (Connecticut)	**1636–37** Dutch Tulipmania crash
1636–38 Pequot War; colonists, assisted by Mohegans, defeat Pequots	
1637 Marquette and Jolliet explore Great Lakes, Mississippi River	
1638 Anne Hutchinson banished from Massachusetts for heresy	
1638 New Sweden founded (Delaware)	
1638 Smallpox epidemic devastates New England Indian tribes	**1639** Portuguese expelled from Japan, replaced by Dutch
	1641 René Descartes' *Discourse*
	1642–48 English Civil War between Royalists and Parliament
	1642 Rembrandt's *The Night Watch*
	1643 "Sun King" Louis XIV of France crowned
1648 Bostgon coopers, shoemakers form guilds	**1648** Potala Palace completed in Lhasa, Tibet
	1649 Cromwell's Parliamentary forces victorious; King Charles I executed
	1649–53 England becomes a Commonwealth (Republic)
	1649–50 Cromwell suppresses Royalists, Catholics in Ireland
c 1650 Iroquois defeat Shawnees and conquer Illinois country; Lakota driven onto Great Plains	
	1652 Tea arrives in England
	1652–74 Anglo-Dutch wars
	1653 Shah Jehan completes Taj Mahal at Agra, India
	1653 Cromwell becomes dictator
1654 Jewish settlers arrive in New Amsterdam from Brazil	
	1660 Restoration of Charles II

AMERICA	ABROAD
	1661–65 Clarendon Codes lead to migration of religious dissenters from England to colonies
	1662 Portugal cedes Bombay to England
1663 Rhode Island gets charter from Charles II enshrining freedom of religion	
1664 Stuyvesant's Dutch defeated by English; New Amsterdam becomes New York	**1664–65** Last Great Plague of England
	1664 Ottomans take Hungary
1664 Sir George Carteret and Lord Berkeley found New Jersey colonies:	

"No man, nor number of men upon Earth hath power or authority to rule over men's consciences in religious matters."
CHARTER OF WEST JERSEY, 1665

	1666 Great Fire of London
	1667 Milton's *Paradise Lost*
	1668 English pirate Henry Morgan captures Panama City
1672 Charles II of England forbids enslavement of Indians	
	1674 Jan Sobieski, future savior of Vienna, elected King of Poland
1675–76 King Philip's (Metacom's) War: Indian uprising against settlers:	

"Thus we were butchered by those merciless heathen."
MARY ROWLANDSON'S *NARRATIVE* OF CAPTIVITY

1676 Nathaniel Bacon, anti-Indian planter, leads rebellion in Virginia, burns Jamestown:

"Damn my blood, I'll kill Governor, Council, Assembly and all!"

	1677 John Bunyan's *The Pilgrim's Progress*
1679 New Hampshire secedes from Massachusetts	**1679** Habeus Corpus Act, England
	1679 Dodo bird on Mauritius becomes extinct
1680 Pueblo Indians revolt, drive Spanish from Santa Fe	

AMERICA	ABROAD
1681 Quaker William Penn given charter for Pennsylvania **1682** La Salle claims Mississippi River Valley for France	
	1683 Ottoman Turks defeated at Vienna; Viennese baker invents "croissant" in celebration **1685** Revocation of Edict of Nantes leads to persecution of French
1686 James II creates Dominion of New England, dissolves colonial legislatures	Protestants; many flee to America **1687** Sir Isaac Newton's *Principia Mathematica* **1688** Glorious Revolution of England; Catholic James II deposed
1689 Dominion of New England dissolved, legislatures reinstated	**1689** Protestant William of Orange becomes King of England **1689** English Bill of Rights
1690 King William's War against French and their Indian allies	**1690** John Locke's *Second Treatise on Government* **1690** William III defeats James II at
1692 Salem, Massachusetts, witch trials; 20 executed **1693** College of William and Mary founded	Battle of the Boyne, Ireland **1696** Tsar Peter I ("the Great") inherits Russian throne
1701 Yale College founded	**1701** Pirate Capt. Kidd hanged, London **1702** Death of William III; Queen Anne
1702–13 "Queen Anne's War" (American theater of War of Spanish Succession) **1704** First American newspaper: William Campbell's *News-Letter*, Boston **1704** Deerfield Raid by French and Indians, Massachusetts	ascends throne **1703** Peter the Great founds St. Petersburg **1704** Battle of Blenheim; English victory thwarts Louis XIV's plan for European domination **1704** English capture Gibraltar **1707** Union of England, Scotland, and Wales in United Kingdom of Great Britain **1709** Peter the Great defeats Swedes
1712 New York slave revolt	at Poltava **1714** Fahrenheit makes first mercury thermometer

	1714 George I, Elector of Hanover, becomes King of Great Britain
	1715 First Jacobite rebellion in Scotland on behalf of exiled Catholic
1718 New Orleans founded by French	King James
	1719 Daniel Defoe's *Robinson Crusoe*
1725 First "Kentucky long rifles" built in	**1725** Casanova born
Pennsylvania by German immigrants	**1725** Peter the Great sends Vitus Bering to explore North Pacific
	1726 Jonathan Swift's *Gulliver's Travels*
	1729 Johann Sebastian Bach's
1730–79 Comanches control most of	*St. Matthew Passion*
Texas, battle Utes and Spanish	
1732–58 Benjamin Franklin publishes	
Poor Richard's Almanack:	

"Early to bed and early to rise makes a man healthy, wealthy, and wise."

1732 Gen. James Oglethorpe founds
Georgia colony as buffer against Spanish

1734 Religious "Great Awakening"
begins in Massachusetts:

"Sinners in the Hands of an Angry God"
SERMON BY JONATHAN EDWARDS

1735 Newspaper publisher John Peter
Zenger acquitted of seditious libel
1736 Benjamin Franklin founds Union
Fire Company, first volunteer fire
department in America

1739 John Wesley founds
Methodist Society
1739 War of Jenkins' Ear: Britain

1740–48 "King George's War" (American
theater of War of Austrian Succession)

against Spain
1741 Russian Bering expedition
discovers Alaska
1741 Frederick the Great's Prussia
defeats Maria Theresa's Austria
1745 Second Jacobite Rebellion
in Scotland defeated

1746 College of New Jersey (Princeton
University) founded

1748 Pompeii excavation begins

1749 Benjamin Franklin founds College of Philadelphia (Univ. of Pennsylvania)
1751 Franklin founds Pennsylvania Hospital, America's first
1752 Liberty Bell arrives in Philadelphia from England

1754–56 French and Indian War begins
1754 Columbia University founded as King's College, New York
1755 French defeat Gen. Braddock and Maj. George Washington at Ft. Duquesne

1756–63 French and Indian War becomes American theater of Seven Years War

1757 Massacre of prisoners by French and Indians at Ft. William Henry
1759 British capture Quebec; end of French Empire in America

1748 Montesquieu's *Spirit of Laws*
1749 Henry Fielding's *Tom Jones*

1751 China invades Tibet
1751 Diderot's *Encyclopédie*

1753 Birth of Miguel Hidalgo y Costilla, father of Mexican independence

1755 Dr. Samuel Johnson's great *Dictionary*
1755 Lisbon earthquake kills more than 100,000
1756–63 American fighting leads to Seven Years War, Anglo-French global conflict
1756 Black Hole of Calcutta
1757 British defeat French at Plassey, India

The Road to Revolution

1760–62 Anglo-Cherokee War in Carolinas, Virginia, Georgia

1763 Treaty of Paris ends Seven Years War: Britain gets all French territory east of Mississippi; Spanish cedes Florida to Britain, gets Louisiana
1763 Royal proclamation forbids settlement in Indian lands west of Appalachians
1763–66 Pontiac's Rebellion; Indian uprising in Ohio Valley

1760 George III becomes King of Great Britain
1762 Jean-Jacques Rousseau's *The Social Contract*
1762 Catherine the Great ascends Russian throne

AMERICA	ABROAD

1764–65 Sugar, Stamp, Quartering Acts provoke colonial protests
1765 Stamp Act Congress, New York:

1764 Voltaire's *Philosophical Dictionary*
1765 Sir William Blackstone's *Commentaries on the Laws of England*

"Taxation without Representation is Tyranny"
PATRIOT JAMES OTIS

1766 Stamp Act repealed by Parliament; Declaratory Act asserts right to tax colonies
1767 Daniel Boone explores Kentucky
1767 Charles Mason and Jeremiah Dixon complete survey
1767 Townsend Act imposes duties to pay for defense of colonies
1768 John Dickinson's *The Liberty Song*:

"Then join hand in hand, brave Americans all—
By uniting we stand, by dividing we fall."

1768–74 Russo-Turkish war
1768 First edition of *Encyclopedia Britannica* published
1769 James Watt's steam engine

1769 San Diego, first of 21 Alta California missions, founded by Franciscan Junípero Serra
1770 Boston "Massacre"

1770 Capt. James Cook discovers Botany Bay, Australia

1772 Samuel Adams founds Committee of Correspondence for independence

1772 Mansfield decision: slavery illegal in Great Britain
1772–95 Three Partitions of Poland; end of Polish state

1773 Tea Act and Boston Tea Party

1773–75 Pugachev serf revolt in Russia

1774 First Continental Congress

"The Shot Heard 'round the World"

1775 April 19 battles at Concord and
Lexington spark American Revolution:

"What a glorious morning this is!"
SAMUEL ADAMS

1775 Second Continental Congress;
Gen. George Washington takes
command of Continental Army
1775 Battle of Bunker Hill:

"You men are all marksmen, now don't fire until
you can see the whites of their eyes."
COL. WILLIAM PRESCOTT

1775 US population reaches 2.5 million   *1775* Samuel Johnson's
Taxation no Tyranny:

"How is it that we hear the loudest yelps for liberty
among the drivers of Negroes?"

1776 Adam Smith's *The Wealth
of Nations*
1776 Edward Gibbon's *The Decline
1776 The Declaration of Independence: and Fall of the Roman Empire*

"We hold these truths to be self-evident that all men are created equal, that
they are endowed by their creator with certain inalienable rights."

"We must indeed all hang together, or most assuredly
we shall all hang separately."
BENJAMIN FRANKLIN AT THE SIGNING OF THE DECLARATION

1776 Tom Paine's *Common Sense*:

"Government, even in its best state, is but a necessary evil;
in its worst state, an intolerable one."

1776 American victories at
Ticonderoga, Trenton, Princeton;
defeats at New York

1776 Execution of American spy
Nathan Hale:

"I regret that I have but one life to give to my country."

1777 Tom Paine coins country name
"United States of America"
1777 Continental Congress adopts
Articles of Confederation, combining
colonies into loose federation
1777 American victory at Saratoga
1777 Washington's army camps for
winter at Valley Forge
1778 Cherry Valley (NY), Wyoming
Valley (PA) massacres of settlers by
pro-British Iroquois; Iroquois defeated

1779 John Paul Jones's *Bonhomme
Richard* captures HMS *Serapis*:

1777 Morocco first country to
recognize American independence

1778 France enters war on side
of America

1779 Capt. Cook killed in Hawaii
1779 Spain sides with colonies

"I have not yet begun to fight!"
JONES, ON APPARENT VERGE OF DEFEAT

1779 Jean Baptiste Pointe du Sable,
Haitian fur trader, founds Chicago
1780 Flight of traitor Benedict Arnold;
execution of British spy John Andre

1781 British surrender at Yorktown
effectively ends Revolutionary War
1781 Articles of Confederation ratified
1781 Spanish found Los Angeles
1782 General Washington creates
Badge of Military Merit (Purple Heart)
1783 Treaty of Paris ends American
Revolutionary War; Loyalist Tories flee
to Canada, Bahamas

1780 Catherine the Great sets
up League of Armed Neutrality
against Britain
1780 Austria's Maria Theresa succeeded
by "enlightened despot" Joseph II

1782 British defeat French fleet
at Battle of the Saintes
1783 Potemkin conquers Crimea
for Russia
1783 Treaty of Versailles ends war
between Britain and Franco-Spanish
alliance
1783 Montgolfier brothers fly
hot-air balloon

The Fledgling Republic

1784 Benjamin Franklin invents bifocals, daylight saving time
1785 US adopts decimal system and dollar
1786 Daniel Shays leads armed rebellion in Massachusetts
1787 Constitutional Convention, Philadelphia
1787–88 Federalist Papers, written by Alexander Hamilton, James Madison, and John Jay:

1784 Affair of the Queen's Necklace, court of Versailles, France

1786 Penang Island first British colony in Southeast Asia

"If men were angels, no government would be necessary."

1788 Constitution ratified by all states except Rhode Island, North Carolina

1789 George Washington elected, inaugurated as first president

1790 Philadelphia becomes capital of United States

1792 Founding of New York Stock Exchange
1793 Eli Whitney invents cotton gin

1794 Whiskey Rebellion, Pennsylvania
1794 Congress authorizes US Navy's first six ships

1796 Washington's farewell address:

1788 George III's first episode of madness
1788 *The Times* of London founded
1788 First Fleet of colonists, convicts arrives in Botany Bay, Australia
1789 Mutiny on HMS *Bounty*
1789 Storming of Bastille begins French Revolution
1789 Declaration of the Rights of Man and of the Citizen, Paris

1791 Haiti slave revolt begins
1791 Mozart begins *Requiem*, dies at 35
1792 Mary Wollstonecraft's *A Vindication of the Rights of Woman*
1793 The Terror; Louis XVI and Marie Antoinette of France executed
1793–1802 France at war with Britain

1795 Napoleon Bonaparte's "whiff of grapeshot" disperses Parisian rebels

"The name of AMERICAN, which belongs to you, in your national capacity, must always exalt the just pride of Patriotism, more than any appellation derived from local discriminations."

AMERICA	ABROAD
	1796 Napoleon's Italian campaign
	1796 Edward Jenner develops smallpox
1797 Undeclared naval war against	vaccination
France	
1797 USS *Constitution* "Old Ironsides"	
launched in Boston	
1797–98 Alien and Sedition Acts	
restrict freedom of speech	*1798* Great Rebellion in Ireland against
	British rule
	1799 Coup of 18 Brumaire; Napoleon
	takes power in Paris as First Consul
	1799 Discovery of Rosetta Stone, key to
	Egyptian hieroglyphs

Jeffersonian America

1800 Thomas Jefferson elected president	*1800* Alessandro Volta invents
1800 Nation's capital moved from	electric battery
Philadelphia to Washington, DC	*1800* Spain secretly cedes Louisiana
1800 Alexander Hamilton founds	to France
New York Post, oldest US newspaper	
still in publication	
1800 Library of Congress established	
from Jefferson's private library	
	1801 Union of Great Britain and
1801–15 US war against Barbary	Ireland
Coast pirates:	

"Millions for defense, but not one cent for tribute!"
POPULAR SLOGAN

	1801 Adm. Horatio Nelson destroys
	Danish fleet at Copenhagen
	1801 Toussaint L'Ouverture declares
	Haiti independent
	1801 Tsar Paul I assassinated
	1801 British drive French from Egypt
1802 US Military Academy opens	*1802* Napoleon annexes northern Italy
at West Point, New York:	

"Duty, Honor, Country"
USMA MOTTO

1803 *Marbury v. Madison* establishes principle of Judicial Review:

1803 Henry Shrapnel invents explosive artillery shell

"It is emphatically the province and duty of the judicial department to say what the law is."

1803 Louisiana Purchase: US pays France $15 million for 888,000 sq. miles; US doubles in size

1804 Lewis and Clark Expedition sets out down Ohio River

1804 Alexander Hamilton killed by Vice President Aaron Burr in duel

1805 US Marines storm Barbary capital at Tripoli

1804 Napoleon crowns himself French emperor; promulgates Code Napoleon

1804 Beethoven's *Eroica* symphony

1805 William Wordsworth's *Prelude*

1805 Napoleon defeats Austro-Russian armies at Austerlitz

1805 Nelson routs French, Spanish fleets at Trafalgar

1806 Zebulon Pike expedition to Rocky Mountains

1807 Chesapeake-Leopard incident off Virginia coast brings US and Britain to brink of war

1807 First Embargo Act bans US trade with foreign nations

1807 Robert Fulton's paddle steamer *Clermont* sails on Hudson

1808 Importation of slaves outlawed

1806 Napoleon enters Berlin, Warsaw

1807 Britain bans slave trade

1807 First gas street lighting in London

1808 Napoleon occupies Spain

1808 Goethe's *Faust*

1808 Portuguese court relocates to Brazil

1808 Beethoven's *5th, 6th Symphonies*

1809 Ft. Wayne Treaty; Shawnee chiefs sell two million acres to US

1809 Tecumseh's Rebellion begins against settler encroachments:

"Burn their dwellings—destroy their stock—slay their wives and children that their very breed may perish! War now! War always! War on the living! War on the dead!"
TECUMSEH (KILLED IN BATTLE OF THAMES, 1813)

	1810 Hidalgo founds Independence movement, Mexico
	1811 First Luddite attacks on machinery, Nottingham
1812–15 War of 1812 against Britain	**1812** British liberate Spain from French rule
1812–14 US Navy frigate battles against Royal Navy:	**1812** Napoleon invades Russia, retreats from Moscow

"Don't give up the ship!"
CAPT. JAMES LAWRENCE OF THE USS *CHESAPEAKE*, MORTALLY WOUNDED

1813–14 Creek War in Florida	**1813** Viennese waltz storms Europe
1813 US invasion of Canada repulsed	**1813** Jane Austen's *Pride and Prejudice*
1813 Oliver H. Perry defeats British on Lake Erie:	**1813** Mexican Congress, called by José Morelos, issues decree of independence

"We have met the enemy, and they are ours."

	1814 Napoleon abdicates; exiled to Elba
1814 British bombardment of Ft. McHenry inspires Francis Scott Key's "Star Spangled Banner":	**1814** Borobudur Temple complex excavated, Java

"By the dawn's early light...our flag was still there."

1814 British capture Washington, DC, burn White House, Capitol	
1815 Treaty of Ghent ends war with Britain	**1815** Congress of Vienna
1815 Battle of New Orleans won by Gen. Andrew Jackson	**1815** Napoleon returns for 100 days; defeated by Wellington at Waterloo
	1815 Napoleon exiled to St. Helena; French monarchy restored
	1817 British defeat Maratha Empire in India
1817–18 Andrew "Long Knife" Jackson invades Florida, wins First Seminole War	**1818** José de San Martín defeats Spanish, wins independence of Chile
	1818 Zulu king Shaka conquers much of southern Africa
1819 Spain cedes Florida to the US	**1819** Lord Byron's *Don Juan*

The Jacksonian Era

1820 Missouri Compromise concerning slavery in new states averts civil war
1820 US naval hero Stephen Decatur killed in duel:

1820 Death of George III

"Our Country! In her intercourse with foreign nations, may she always be in the right, but our country, right or wrong!"
DECATUR'S TOAST TO AMERICA

1820 Birth of Susan B. Anthony, campaigner for abolition, temperance, women's suffrage
1820 Washington Irving's *Legend of Sleepy Hollow* and *Rip van Winkle*
1820 Liberia founded as US colony for freed slaves

1821–22 Denmark Vesey slave rebellion

1822 Mexico takes over California

1823 Monroe Doctrine asserted:

1821 Peru, Mexico, Central America, independent from Spain
1821 Keats dies in Rome at 26
1821–29 Greek struggle for independence from Ottoman Turks
1821–22 Simón Bolívar liberates Venezuela from Spain
1822 Prince Pedro declares independence of Brazil, and himself Emperor Pedro I

"The American continents...are henceforth not to be considered as subjects for future colonization by any European powers."

1825 Erie Canal opened
1826 James Fenimore Cooper's *Last of the Mohicans*
1828 Andrew Jackson elected President
1828 Noah Webster's *American Dictionary*

1825–26 Decembrist rising in Russia

1827 Franco-Russo-British fleet defeats Turks at Navarino

1829 Slavery abolished in Mexico
1829 British suppress *sati* (widow-burning) in India
1829 Stevenson's *Rocket* first modern locomotive

AMERICA	ABROAD

1830 Daniel Webster debates Robert Hayne:

1830 Paris revolution; Charles X overthrown; Louis Philippe takes throne

"Liberty and Union, now and forever, one and inseparable!"
WEBSTER

1830 Book of Mormon presented by Joseph Smith

1831 First US railroad station, Baltimore
1831 Southeast Indian relocations
1831 Nat Turner slave revolt:

1830 Ecuador secedes from Colombia
1830 Polish revolt against Russian rule
1830 France invades, colonizes Algeria
1831 Belgium gains independence from Netherlands

"I saw white spirits and black spirits engaged in battle, and the sun was darkened—the thunder rolled in the heavens, and blood flowed in streams."
TURNER

1831 William Lloyd Garrison founds *The Liberator*, abolitionist newspaper
1832 Black Hawk War, Wisconsin; Sauk and Fox tribes massacred
1832 Nullification Crisis; South Carolina threatens to secede if federal government enforces tariffs:

1831 Voyage of Darwin's *Beagle*
1831 French Foreign Legion formed
1832 Giuseppe Mazzini founds Young Italy movement
1832 Great Reform Bill, Great Britain
1832 Great cholera epidemic in Europe and North America

"Disunion by armed force is treason."
ANDREW JACKSON

1834 Cyrus McCormick patents reaper

1835 Samuel Colt invents revolver:

1833 Alexander Pushkin's *Eugene Onegin*
1834 Slavery abolished throughout British Empire
1834 Carlist civil wars begin in Spain

"God made men equal; Sam Colt keeps them that way."
POPULAR SAYING

1835–42 Second Seminole War
1835 P. T. Barnum's circus first tour

1835 Alexis de Tocqueville publishes *Democracy in America*

America	Abroad
	1835 Louis Daguerre creates daguerreotype photograph
	1835 Hans Christian Andersen publishes first children's stories
1836 Texas declares independence from Mexico; Alamo falls:	**1836** Boers begin Great Trek

"The victory will cost the enemy so dear,
that it will be worse for him than a defeat."
COL. TRAVIS, COMMANDER OF THE ALAMO

"Remember the Alamo!"
BATTLE CRY OF SAM HOUSTON AT SAN JACINTO

America	Abroad
1836–45 Texas an independent republic	
1837 John Deere develops steel plow	**1837** Queen Victoria crowned
1837 Horace Mann becomes Massachusetts Secretary of Education:	**1837** Dickens's *Oliver Twist*

"Education...is the great equalizer of the conditions of men."

America	Abroad
1837–40 Texas Rangers battle Comanches	
1838 Underground Railway smuggles runaway slaves to freedom	**1838–42** First Anglo-Afghan war
1838 Trail of Tears: 4,000 Cherokee die in forcible relocation to Oklahoma	
1838 Frederick Douglass escapes to Massachusetts	
1839 *Amistad* mutiny	**1839** Bicycle invented, Scotland
1839 Abner Doubleday lays out first baseball diamond	**1839** First Opium War between Britain and China
	1840 First British Colonists arrive in New Zealand
	1842 Hong Kong ceded in perpetuity to Britain by China
1843 Great Migration to Oregon	
1844 Samuel Morse sends message on his telegraph:	**1844** Alexandre Dumas's *The Three Musketeers*

"What Hath God Wrought?"
MORSE'S FIRST TELEGRAM FROM WASHINGTON TO BALTIMORE

1845 Annexation of Texas:

'"[It is] our manifest destiny to overspread…the whole of the continent."
JOHN L. O'SULLIVAN

1845 Oregon Treaty settles border
with Canada
1845 US Naval Academy founded
at Annapolis
1845 Frederick Douglass's *Narrative
of the Life of Frederick Douglass,
American Slave*:

1845–9 Anglo-Sikh wars, Punjab

"The soul that is within me no man can degrade."

1846 Smithsonian Institution founded
1846–47 Donner Party stranded
1846–48 Mexican-American War
1847 Brigham Young leads Mormons
to Great Salt Lake
1847 US captures Mexico City

1846–49 Potato blight causes
Great Hunger famine in Ireland
1847 Thackeray's *Vanity Fair*
1847 Liberian independence from US

A House Divided

1848 Seneca Falls Women's
Rights Convention:

1848 Year of Revolutions across Europe

"We hold these truths to be self-evident:
that all men and women are created equal."
ELIZABETH CADY STANTON'S DECLARATION OF SENTIMENTS

1848 Treaty of Guadalupe Hidalgo:
US gains from Mexico include
California, Nevada, Arizona, Utah
1848 Stephen Foster composes
"Oh Susannah"

1848 Karl Marx, Friedrich Engels write
Communist Manifesto

1849 California Gold Rush

1849 British conquer Punjab

1849 Longfellow's "The Building of the Ship":

"Thou, too, sail on, O Ship of State! / Sail on, O Union, strong and great! / Humanity with all its fears, / With all the hopes of future years, / Is hanging breathless on thy fate!"

1849 Anti-Catholic, anti-immigrant "Know-Nothing" movement founded
1850 Pinkerton founds Detective Agency
1850 Nathaniel Hawthorne's *The Scarlet Letter*
1850 Great Compromise postpones Southern secession; admits California as a free state in return for passage of Fugitive Slave Act:

1850–62 Taiping Rebellion, China

"We are not a nation, but a union, a confederacy of equal and sovereign states."
JOHN C. CALHOUN

"Go West, young man, and grow up with the country."
HORACE GREELEY

1851 Melville's *Moby Dick*
1851 Isaac Singer's sewing machine
1852 Harriet Beecher Stowe's *Uncle Tom's Cabin*
1854 Kansas-Nebraska Act breaks Missouri Compromise, leads to founding of Republican Party and Bleeding Kansas War
1854 Henry David Thoreau's *Walden*:

1851 Giuseppe Verdi's *Rigoletto*
1851 Louis Napoleon's coup d'état, France; becomes Emperor Napoleon III

1854–56 Crimean War; Russians defeated by Turks, British, French

"The mass of men lead lives of quiet desperation."

1854 Commodore Matthew Perry's fleet of "black ships" forces opening of Japan to Western trade

1854 Charge of the Light Brigade, Balaclava, Crimea

1855 Walt Whitman publishes
Leaves of Grass:

"The United States themselves are essentially the greatest poem."

1855 Longfellow's *Song of Hiawatha*

1856 Gustave Flaubert's
Madame Bovary

1857 Supreme Court's "Dred Scott"
decision denies blacks US citizenship
1857–58 Mormon-US war

1857–58 Sepoy Mutiny against
British rule in India
1858 Chechnya subdued by Russia
1859 Charles Darwin's *On the
Origin of Species*

1859 John Brown's raid on Harper's
Ferry Federal Arsenal:

1859 J.S. Mill's essay *On Liberty*
1859 France, Sardinia, defeat Austria;
creation of Italian state

"Now, if it is deemed necessary that I should forfeit my life for the
furtherance of the ends of justice, and mingle my blood further with
the blood of my children and with the blood of millions in this
slave country whose rights are disregarded by wicked, cruel,
and unjust enactments—I submit, so let it be done!"
BROWN'S LAST SPEECH BEFORE HIS EXECUTION

Civil War: The Last Full Measure of Devotion

1860 Abraham Lincoln elected
1860 Pony Express launched
1861 Southern states secede;
Jefferson Davis elected president
of Confederacy
1861 Civil War begins with South
Carolina attack on Ft. Sumter
1862 Homestead Act offers 160 acres of
free federal land to Western settlers
1862 Battles of Antietam, Second Bull
Run, Fredericksburg, Shiloh:

1860 Victor Emmanuel proclaimed
King of Italy by Garibaldi
1861 Tsar Alexander II abolishes
serfdom in Russia

1862 Bismarck becomes Prussian
Prime Minister

"It is well that war is so terrible—lest we should grow too fond of it."
ROBERT E. LEE, SEEING THE FEDERAL ASSAULT DISSOLVE AT FREDERICKSBURG

1862 Medal of Honor established
by Congress
1863 Emancipation Proclamation:

"All persons held as slaves within any state...in rebellion against the United
States, shall be then, thenceforward, and forever free."

"No more auction block for me, no more no more!"
SLAVE SONG

1863 Battles of Chancellorsville, | **1863** French invade Mexico, install
Gettysburg, Vicksburg, Chickamauga, | Archduke Maximilian as emperor
Chattanooga; Confederacy split in two:

"Lincoln's coming with his chariot coming to carry me home."
SPIRITUAL IMPROVISED BY MARYLAND SLAVES WATCHING
ARMY OF POTOMAC MARCH TO GETTYSBURG

1863 Death of "Stonewall" Jackson:

"Let us cross over the river and rest under the shade of the trees."
JACKSON'S LAST WORDS

1863 New York City Draft Riots:
Irish immigrant mobs lynch
free blacks
1864 Battles of Spotsylvania Court
House, Cold Harbor:

"I propose to fight it out on this line, if it takes all summer."
ULYSSES S. GRANT TELEGRAM TO WAR DEPARTMENT FROM COLD HARBOR

1864 Sherman burns Atlanta, | **1864** Prussian-Danish war
reaches sea:

"War is the remedy our enemies have chosen,
and I say let us give them all they want."

1864 International Red Cross founded
in Switzerland
1864 Louis Pasteur invents
pasteurization

AMERICA	ABROAD
1865 Congress passes 13th Amendment, abolishing slavery	*1865* Lewis Carroll's *Alice's Adventures in Wonderland*
1865 Lee surrenders at Appomatox; Confederacy defeated	*1865* Joseph Lister pioneers antiseptics
1865 Lincoln's second inauguration:	

"With malice toward none, with charity for all...let us strive on to finish the work we are in...to do all which may achieve and cherish a just and a lasting peace."

1865 Transatlantic telegraph cable completed; connects New, Old Worlds
1865 Lincoln assassinated by John Wilkes Booth

Reconstruction: Promise & Betrayal

1865–76 Reconstruction and military occupation of South; Black Codes	
1866–75 Armed White League insurrections in South	*1866* Alfred Nobel invents dynamite
1866 Civil Rights Act passed over Pres. Andrew Johnson's veto	*1866* Austria defeated by Prussia; Italy gains Venice
1866 Red Cloud's Sioux close Bozeman Trail; wipe out Fetterman detatchment	
1866–90 Indian Wars	
1866 Formal foundation of Ku Klux Klan, Tennessee	

1867 9th, 10th Cavalry—black "Buffalo Soldiers"—recruited, sent West
1867 Seward's folly: Alaska bought from Russia for $7.2 million
1867 Horatio Alger's *Ragged Dick*
1867 Howard University founded
1867 First cattle drive from Texas to Abilene, Kansas, up Chisholm Trail

1867 Diamonds discovered in South Africa
1867 Canada becomes self-governing dominion
1867 End of Tokugawa Shogunate in Japan; Meiji Emperor restored
1867 Emperor Maximilian executed in Mexico City
1867 Karl Marx's *Das Kapital*

AMERICA	ABROAD
1868 14th Amendment extends equal protection to States	*1868* British punitive expedition in Ethiopia
1868 Cornelius Vanderbilt battles Jay Gould, James Fisk for Erie Railroad	
1868 Impeachment trial of Andrew Johnson	
1869 Golden Spike completes Transcontinental Railroad	*1869* Suez Canal opens
	1869 Leo Tolstoy's *War and Peace*
1869 Knights of Labor founded	
1870 15th Amendment (voting rights)	
1870 John D. Rockefeller founds Standard Oil	*1870–71* Franco-Prussian War
1871 US Navy Korean Campaign	*1871* Paris Commune, Fall of
1871 National Rifle Association founded	Napoleon III
1871 Los Angeles race riots against Chinese immigrant workers	*1871* Wilhelm of Prussia crowned German Emperor at Versailles
1871 Downfall of Tammany leader Boss Tweed, New York City	*1871* Henry Morton Stanley finds missing explorer David Livingstone
1871 Great Chicago Fire	in the Congo
1872 Yellowstone first National Park	
1872 Victoria Woodhull first woman to run for presidential office	
1873 Financial Panic	*1873* Zanzibar abolishes slave trade
1873 Winchester 73 Repeating Rifle, "Gun that Won the West"	
1873 Levi Strauss patents riveted blue jeans	
1874 Joseph Glidden patents barbed wire	*1874* Degas organizes first Impressionist Exhibition, Paris
1875 Black Hills Gold Rush provokes war with Sioux and Cheyenne	
1876 Alexander Graham Bell patents telephone:	*1876* Bulgarian April Uprising; massacres by Turks

"Mr. Watson, come here. I want you!"
FIRST TELEPHONE CONVERSATION

1876 Custer's Last Stand—Sioux wipe out US cavalry at Little Big Horn
1876 Wild Bill Hickock murdered holding "dead man's hand"

AMERICA	ABROAD

1877 Disputed election; Rutherford B. Hayes president; Reconstruction ends

1877 Porfirio Díaz becomes dictator of Mexico:

"Poor Mexico, so far from God, and so close to the United States."

Industrialization & the End of the Frontier

1877 Nez Percé War:

"From where the sun now stands, I shall fight no more forever."
CHIEF JOSEPH, UPON SURRENDERING TO US SOLDIERS

1877 Great Railway Strike crushed by Federal troops
1879 Mary Baker Eddy founds Christian Science church
1879–1935 Life of Will Rogers:

1878–80 British win Second Afghan War
1879 Anglo-Zulu War

"What the country needs is dirtier fingernails and cleaner minds."

1879 Edison's light bulb

1881 Tuskegee Institute founded
1881 Billy the Kid shot dead by Sheriff Pat Garrett
1881 Gunfight at OK Corral, Arizona
1881 Pres. James Garfield assassinated

1880 Ned Kelly hanged in Australia
1881–84 Anti-Jewish pogroms in Russia
1881 Assassination of Tsar Alexander II

1882–1943 Chinese Exclusion Act restricts Chinese immigration and eligibility for citizenship
1882 US ratifies Geneva Convention
1882 Oscar Wilde lectures to miners in Leadville, CO, during coast-to-coast US tour
1883 Brooklyn Bridge completed
1884 John Singer Sargent paints *Madame X*
1884 Mark Twain's *Huckleberry Finn*

1882 Egypt becomes British protectorate
1882 Gottleib Daimler invents internal combustion engine, Germany

1883 Krakatoa volcano explodes
1884–1954 France takes control of Indochina

1885 Karl Benz builds first gasoline-fueled automobile

	1885 King Leopold of Belgium takes ownership of Congo
1886 Apache leader Geronimo surrenders to Gen. Crook:	**1886** Slavery abolished in Cuba

"Once I moved about like the wind. Now I surrender to you and that is all."

1886 Statue of Liberty dedicated by Pres. Grover Cleveland
1886 Samuel Gompers founds American Federation of Labor
1886 General Strike and Haymarket Riot, Chicago
1886 Coca-Cola invented

1887 China's Yellow River bursts banks, kills one million people
1888 Vincent van Gogh's *Sunflowers*
1889 Oklahoma Land Rush on land pledged to Indians

1889 Eiffel Tower opens, Paris
1889 Brazil deposes emperor, becomes Republic
1889 Nietzsche's *Twilight of the Idols*

1890 Sitting Bull killed by reservation police
1890 Massacre of Sioux at Wounded Knee, Dakota Territory
1890 Emily Dickinson's *Poems*
1890 Jacob Riis's *How the Other Half Lives*
1890 John D. Rockefeller founds University of Chicago
1890 Sherman Antitrust Act enacted to break up monopolies

1890–1947 Meiji Constitution, Japan

1891 Dr. James Naismith invents basketball at Springfield, MA, YMCA
1891 Edison invents Kinetoscope, motion-picture camera
1891 Hamburger invented in Tulsa
1892 Peak of lynching wave in the South; 161 blacks killed
1892 Ellis Island opens to receive immigrants

1891 Beginning of Trans-Siberian Railroad

1892 Rudolf Diesel patents engine

AMERICA	ABROAD
1892 Homestead Strike against Carnegie Steel company defeated	
1893 Historian Frederick Jackson Turner announces "closing of frontier"	**1893** New Zealand gives women the vote
1893 Americans take control of Hawaii	**1894** Capt. Alfred Dreyfus falsely accused of espionage in France
1894 Pullman Strike in Chicago broken by federal troops	**1895** Guglielmo Marconi transmits radio messages
1895 Stephen Crane's *The Red Badge of Courage*	**1895** Trials of Oscar Wilde
	1895–98 Cuban rebellion against Spain (independence 1902)
1896 William Jennings Bryan's "Cross of Gold" speech at Democratic National Convention:	**1896** Abyssinians humiliate Italian Army at Adowa

"You shall not press down upon the brow of labor this crown of thorns, you shall not crucify mankind upon a cross of gold."

AMERICA	ABROAD
1896 *Plessy v. Ferguson* upholds "separate but equal"	**1896** First modern Olympic Games at Athens
1896–1901 Butch Cassidy and the Sundance Kid lead Wild Bunch bank robberies	**1896** Klondike Gold Rush
1897 Boston subway, first in US	**1897** Queen Victoria Diamond Jubilee

The Emergence of a New World Power

1898 Spanish-American War:

"Remember the Maine and to hell with Spain!"
US WAR CRY

AMERICA	ABROAD
1898 Spain cedes Puerto Rico, Guam, and the Philippines to the US:	**1898** Boxer Rebellion in China against foreigners, Christians

"It has been a splendid little war, begun with the highest motives... favored by that fortune which loves the brave."
SECRETARY OF STATE JOHN HAY

AMERICA	ABROAD
1898 City of Brooklyn annexed by New York	**1898** Battle of Omdurman; Anglo-Egyptian reconquest of Sudan

AMERICA	ABROAD

1898 US formally annexes Hawaii

1898 Marie and Pierre Curie discover radium
1899–1902 Second Anglo-Boer War, South Africa

1899–1913 Philippine Insurrection:

"Underneath the starry flag, civilize 'em with a Krag."
US ARMY SONG ABOUT PHILIPPINE WAR

1899 Scott Joplin's "Maple Leaf Rag"
1899 Samoan Campaign; US obtains Eastern Samoa
1900–1901 China Relief Expedition; US joins suppression of Boxer Rebellion
1901 Pres. William McKinley assassinated
1901 Oil strike at Spindletop, Texas
1901 Theodore Roosevelt becomes president:

1900 King Umberto I of Italy assassinated
1900 Joseph Conrad's *Heart of Darkness*
1901 Death of Queen Victoria

"I have always been fond of the West African proverb:
Speak softly and carry a big stick; you will go far."

1901 Birth of Louis "Satchmo" Armstrong
1901 Booker T. Washington writes *Up From Slavery*, dines at White House

1903 Wright brothers achieve first powered, manned flight
1903 Baseball's first World Series
1903 W.E.B. DuBois's *The Souls of Black Folk*
1904 US acquires Panama Canal Zone; Roosevelt orders "Make the dirt fly"

1902 Rhodes Scholarship established by Cecil Rhodes's estate
1903 Kishinev Pogrom in Russia

1904 Freud's *Psychopathology of Everyday Life*
1904–5 Japan wins war against Russia
1904 British military expedition reaches Lhasa, Tibet
1904–7 German genocide of Herero tribe, South-West Africa
1905 Revolution in Russia

1905 Edith Wharton's *House of Mirth*

1906 San Francisco earthquake and fire

1905 Einstein develops Theory of Relativity
1906 HMS *Dreadnought*, first modern battleship, sparks naval arms race

1907 Belgian chemist Leo Baekeland invents plastics

1908 Term "melting pot" first used to describe effects of immigration:

1908 Baden-Powell founds Boy Scout movement, England

"America is God's Crucible, the great Melting-Pot where all the races of Europe are melting and reforming."
ISRAEL ZANGWILL

1908 Model T Ford goes into production in Detroit:

"You can paint it any color, so long as it's black."
HENRY FORD

1909 NAACP founded
1909 Adm. Robert E. Peary expedition to North Pole

1910 Japan occupies Korea
1910 Mexican Revolution begins
1910–13 Doomed Scott Anatarctic expedition

1911 John Browning designs Colt .45 automatic pistol
1911 Triangle Shirtwaist fire, New York
1911 Rockefeller's Standard Oil broken up
1911 First Indianapolis 500 race
1911 Hiram Bingham discovers Macchu Picchu; first great US archaeological triumph

1911–12 Chinese Revolution led by Dr. Sun Yat-sen; end of Manchu Dynasty
1912 *Titanic* hits iceberg and sinks

1913 New York Armory art show; first exhibition of modern art in US
1914 Panama Canal opens
1914 Immigration reaches all time high of 1.2 million per year
1914 Great Migration northward of Southern Blacks begins

1914 Assassination of Archduke Franz Ferdinand at Sarajevo

1914–18 Pres. Woodrow Wilson sends troops to Nicaragua, Haiti, Cuba, etc.:

1914–18 First World War; nine million killed on battlefield

"I am going to teach the South American republics to elect good men."

1915 German- and Irish-American groups oppose aid to Western Allies:

1915 Genocide of Armenians in Ottoman Turkey

"There is no room in this country for hyphenated Americanism."
PRES. THEODORE ROOSEVELT

1915 German U–boat torpedoes civilian liner *Lusitania*, kills 128 Americans
1915–34 US troops in Haiti
1916–17 Gen. Pershing leads expedition to Mexico in pursuit of Pancho Villa

1917 Unrestricted German submarine warfare takes toll on US ships
1917 Wilson declares war on Germany:

1915 Germans initiate use of poison gas on Western Front

1916 Battles of the Somme, Jutland, Verdun
1916 Easter Rising, Dublin
1917 Zimmerman Telegram reveals plans for German-Mexican alliance against US

"The world must be made safe for democracy."

1917 Puerto Ricans gain US citizenship
1917 US purchases Danish Virgin Islands
1917 Selective Service Act begins draft
1917 First jazz recording, "Livery Stable Blues"
1917 American Expeditionary Force arrives in France:

1917 French army mutinies
1917 Lawrence of Arabia leads Arab revolt against Turks
1917 Third battle of Ypres
1917 Russian Revolution

"Lafayette, we are here."
LT. COL. CHARLES STANTON AT JULY 4TH PARADE IN PARIS

1918 *Stars and Stripes* newspaper begins publication

1918–22 Russian Civil war

1918 Americans defeat Germans at Belleau Wood, Meuse-Argonne, Marne:

"Come on, you sons of bitches, do you want to live forever?"
GUNNERY SGT. DANIEL DALY EXHORTING WEARY MARINES TO ATTACK AT BELLEAU WOOD

1918 Wilson's "Fourteen Points" for peace include principle of self-determination:

1918 German Spring Offensive defeated

"Mr. Wilson bores me with his Fourteen Points!
Why, God Almighty has only ten!"
GEORGES CLEMENCEAU, FRENCH PRIME MINISTER

1918 Armistice, 11 A.M., November 11
1918–19 Great Influenza Pandemic kills 500,000 in US; 20–40 million worldwide
1918–21 US in Allied intervention against Bolsheviks; GIs sent to Archangel, Murmansk, Vladivostok
1919 American Legion founded
1919 Black Sox scandal; fixing of World Series

1918 Germany surrenders to Allies; Kaiser abdicates

1919–33 Weimar Republic, Germany
1919 Treaty of Versailles
1919 League of Nations founded
1919 Ernest Rutherford, New Zealand scientist, splits atom
1919–21 Irish War of Independence
1919–22 Greco-Turkish War; Greeks massacred at Smyrna

1920 19th Amendment; women win right to vote
1920–33 Prohibition

1921 Quota Act limits immigration
1921 Tulsa race riot
1922 T.S. Eliot's *The Waste Land*

1920 British form Iraq out of three Mesopotamian provinces of former Ottoman Empire
1921 Hitler becomes leader of Germany's Nazi Party
1922 League of Nations gives Middle East Mandates to Britain and France
1922 Mussolini marches on Rome, becomes dictator
1922 Irish Free State established; Irish Civil War begins
1922 Murder of Walter Rathenau by German right-wing extremists

AMERICA	ABROAD
	1922 Howard Carter discovers Tutenkhamen's tomb, Egypt
1923 Robert Frost's Pulitzer Prize–winning *New Hampshire*	**1923** Great Kanto Earthquake, Japan, kills 140,000
	1923 Failed Beer Hall Putsch by Nazis, Munich
	1923 Kemal Atatürk founds Turkish Republic, begins secular reforms
1924 American Indians become US Citizens	**1924** Death of Lenin; Stalin takes power in Soviet Union
1924 Gershwin's "Rhapsody in Blue"	
1924 IBM founded	
1925 Scopes "Monkey Trial"	
1925 F. Scott Fitzgerald's *The Great Gatsby*	
1926 Ernest Hemingway's *The Sun Also Rises*	**1926** Ibn Saud, first king of Saudi Arabia
1927 Execution of anarchists Sacco and Vanzetti	**1927** Black Friday collapse, Germany
1927 Duke Ellington plays at Cotton Club, Harlem	**1927** Josephine Baker the toast of Paris
1927 Babe Ruth hits 60 home runs in a single season	**1927** Marcel Proust's *À la recherche du temps perdu*
1927 Al Jolson in *The Jazz Singer*; first "talkie" motion picture	
1927 Charles Lindbergh makes first nonstop solo flight across Atlantic in *Spirit of St. Louis*	
1928 Paul Robeson records "Ol' Man River"	**1928** Alexander Fleming discovers penicillin, antibiotics

The Depression & the Age of Dictators

1929 Great Stock Market Crash:

"Wall Street Lays an Egg"
VARIETY HEADLINE, OCTOBER 30, 1929

1929 Gangsters in St. Valentine's Day Massacre, Chicago	**1929–2000** PRI party in power in Mexico

1929–40 Great Depression:

"Brother, can you spare a dime?"
POPULAR SONG

1930 Hays Code of movie censorship	**1930** Gandhi's Salt March, India
1930 Edward Hopper paints *Early Sunday Morning*	**1931** New Delhi replaces Calcutta as capital of India
1931 Empire State Building tallest in world	**1931** Japan invades Manchuria
1931 First woman elected senator, Hattie Caraway of Arkansas	
1931 Gangster Al Capone convicted of tax evasion:	

"My rackets are run on strictly American lines."

1932 "Bonus Army" of WWI veterans attacked by Douglas MacArthur's troops in Washington, DC	**1932** Aldous Huxley's *Brave New World*
1932 Franklin Delano Roosevelt elected president in a landslide:	**1932** Iraq becomes independent from British Mandate

"I pledge you, I pledge myself, to a new deal for the American people."
ROOSEVELT ON ACCEPTING NOMINATION

"The only thing we have to fear is fear itself."
INAUGURAL ADDRESS

1932 Lindbergh baby kidnapped in "crime of the century"	**1932–33** Collectivization famine in Ukraine, USSR
1933 Hundred Days (New Deal legislation)	**1933** Hitler elected German Chancellor; Reichstag fire
1933 Refugees from Nazi Germany, including Albert Einstein, arrive in US	**1933** Nazis begin book-burning, open concentration camps
1933 "Good Neighbor" policy towards Latin American countries	
1933 Prohibition repealed by 21st Amendment:	

"Beer by Easter!"
SLOGAN

AMERICA	ABROAD

1933–34 Glass-Steagall Act, SEC established
1934 Solo debut of Ella Fitzgerald at Harlem's Apollo Theater
1935 Populist Louisiana governor Huey Long assassinated:

1934 Hitler becomes Führer of Third Reich
1935 Nuremberg anti-Semitic laws passed

"Every man a king!"
LONG'S SLOGAN

1935 Works Progress Administration; Social Security program
1935 Wagner National Labor Relations Act protects union rights
1935 Hoover Dam completed
1936 Jesse Owens wins four gold medals at Berlin Olympics

1935 Italy invades Abyssinia
1935–39 USSR Great Purge; Moscow Show trials

1936 Nazi Germany invades "demilitarized" Rhineland
1936–39 Spanish Civil War
1936 Pablo Picasso's *Guernica*

1937 King of Delta Blues Robert Johnson's *Cross Road Blues*
1937 Golden Gate Bridge opens
1937 Fire destroys Hindenburg airship, New Jersey:

1937 Japan invades China: Rape of Nanking
1937 Nazi Germany annexes Austria

"Oh the humanity!"
RADIO EYEWITNESS REPORT BY HERBERT MORRISON

1937 Aviator Amelia Earhart disappears over Pacific
1938 Samuel Barber's "Adagio for Strings"
1938 Wallace Carothers invents nylon
1938 Joe "Brown Bomber" Louis knocks out Germany's Max Schmeling
1938 US Highway 66 between Chicago and LA, the "Mother Road," completed:

1938 Nazis occupy Sudetenland in Czechoslovakia
1938 Nazi *Kristallnacht* (Night of Broken Glass)
1938 "Peace in our time"; appeasement at Munich by British prime minister Chamberlain

"Get your kicks on Route 66."
NAT KING COLE HIT, 1946

The "Greatest Generation" & the War Years

1939 John Steinbeck's *The Grapes of Wrath*
1939 *The Wizard of Oz; Gone With the Wind; Stagecoach*
1939 Billie Holliday performs "Strange Fruit"
1939 Lou Gehrig, Pride of the Yankees, retires from baseball:

1939 Nazi Germany makes "Pact of Steel" with Italy
1939 Spanish Republic defeated; Franco becomes dictator
1939 Nazi-Soviet Pact
1939 Nazis invade Poland; in response Britain and France declare war; World War II begins

"You have been reading about a bad break I got. Yet today I consider myself the luckiest man on the face of this earth."
GEHRIG'S FAREWELL SPEECH

1940 Walt Disney's *Fantasia*
1940 First McDonald's restaurant
1940 Frank Sinatra joins Tommy Dorsey Orchestra, becomes first teen idol

1939 Soviet Union invades Poland
1939–40 Soviet Union occupies Baltic States, invades Finland
1940 Germany, Japan, and Italy form Axis
1940 Blitzkrieg overwhelms France, Holland, Belgium; Dunkirk evacuation
1940 Winston Churchill becomes British prime minister
1940 France falls; Britain alone
1940 Battle of Britain forces delay of German invasion
1940 Leon Trotsky murdered by Stalinists, Mexico City

1941 Lend-Lease Act to assist beleaguered Britain
1941 Mount Rushmore National Memorial completed
1941 Pearl Harbor Attack, December 7; America enters the war:

1941 Hitler invades Soviet Union
1941–44 Siege of Leningrad

"A date which will live in infamy."
FDR

1941 Orson Welles's *Citizen Kane*
1941 Glenn Miller's "Chattanooga Choo Choo"

AMERICA	ABROAD
1942 Fall of Philippines to Japan; Bataan Death March:	**1942** Singapore falls to Japan

"I shall return."
GEN. DOUGLAS MACARTHUR

AMERICA	ABROAD
1942 Victories at Coral Sea, Midway, Guadalcanal **1942** Allies land in North Africa; "Operation Torch" **1942** Bing Crosby's "White Christmas" **1942** *Casablanca* released:	**1942** Wannsee Conference: Nazis plan "Final Solution" to "Jewish question"; extermination of Europe's Jews **1942–45** Holocaust: Nazi death machine slaughters 6 million Jews

"Round up the usual suspects."
CLAUDE RAINS AS CAPT. LOUIS RENAULT

AMERICA	ABROAD
1942–45 Internment of West Coast Japanese-Americans **1942** Zoot Suit riots, Los Angeles **1943** Rodgers and Hammerstein's *Oklahoma!* performed **1943** Detroit race riots **1943** Allies invade Sicily and Italy; fall of Mussolini **1944** D-Day **1944** FDR wins record fourth election **1944** Battle of the Bulge:	**1943** Russians defeat Nazis at Stalingrad, Kursk **1943** Germans and Italians surrender in North Africa **1943** Mussolini overthrown (killed 1945) **1944** Paris liberated by Allies **1944** Warsaw Uprising

"Nuts!"
RESPONSE OF BRIG. GEN. ANTHONY MCAULIFFE
TO GERMAN DEMAND FOR SURRENDER OF 101ST AIRBORNE AT BASTOGNE

AMERICA	ABROAD
1944 IBM ASSC, first digital computer, Harvard University **1944** GI Bill **1944** Battle of Leyte Gulf, largest naval battle in history; MacArthur returns to Philippines **1945** Yalta Conference between FDR, Churchill, Stalin **1945** FDR dies; Harry Truman becomes president **1945** Battles of Iwo Jima, Okinawa	**1945** Auschwitz liberated by Soviets **1945** Russians take Berlin; Germany surrenders

1945 First atomic test, New Mexico: |

"I am become Death, Shatterer of Worlds."
ROBERT OPPENHEIMER, DIRECTOR OF MANHATTAN PROJECT,
QUOTING HINDU SCRIPTURE

1945 Atom bombs dropped on
Hiroshima, Nagasaki; Japan surrenders:

"The force from which the sun draws its power has been loosed against
those who brought war to the Far East."
HARRY S TRUMAN

1945 Germany and Japan occupied
by Allies
1945–6 Nuremberg War Crimes Tribunal
1945 United Nations founded

The Cold War & the Baby Boom

1946 Philippines granted independence
from US
1946 Robert Penn Warren's *All the
King's Men*
1946 *Best Years of Our Lives*
1946 Mother Cabrini first American
to become a saint
1946–57 American baby boom

1946 Juan Peron president of Argentina
1946 Italy a republic

1946 Soviet Union tightens grip on
Eastern Europe:

"From Stettin in the Baltic to Trieste in the Adriatic, an iron curtain
has descended across the continent."
WINSTON CHURCHILL

1947 Jackie Robinson first black Major
League Baseball player
1947 First "Levittown" suburb
1947 Howard Hughes flies *Spruce Goose*,
world's largest airplane
1947 Truman Doctrine and strategy of
containment of communism

1947 India, Pakistan, Burma gain
independence from Britain
1947 Religious massacres, mass
migration in India, Pakistan

AMERICA	ABROAD

1947 Marshall Plan to help rebuild devastated Europe:

1947 UN Partition Plan for Palestine

"Our policy is directed not against any country or doctrine, but against hunger, poverty, desperation, and chaos."
GEN. GEORGE MARSHALL

1947 CIA founded
1947 Chuck Yeager breaks sound barrier, flying at Mach 1
1947 House Committee on Un-American Activities (HUAC) holds first hearings on communism in Hollywood; film studios begin blacklist of allegedly subversive filmmakers
1948 Truman orders desegregation of US Armed Forces

1948 Berlin airlift
1948 State of Israel declared; attacked by Egypt, Lebanon, TransJordan, Iraq, Syria
1948 Mahatma Gandhi assassinated
1948 Apartheid laws enacted in South Africa

1949 Hank Williams records "I'm So Lonely I Could Cry"
1949 Arthur Miller's *Death of a Salesman* produced
1949 NATO founded
1950–53 Korean War begins with North Korean invasion of the South
1950 Debut of *Peanuts* comic strip
1950 Abstract Expressionist Jackson Pollock paints drip painting *One*
1950 Sen. Joe McCarthy claims State Department includes communists, sparks witch hunt
1951 US and allied UN forces push Chinese and North Koreans back to 38th parallel
1951 MacArthur fired by Truman
1951 22nd Amendment limits US presidents to two terms
1951 Marlon Brando in Tennessee Williams's *A Streetcar Named Desire*

1949 Soviets test atomic bomb
1949 Communists take over China; Nationalists flee to Taiwan
1949 George Orwell's *1984*

1950 China occupies Tibet
1950 Pablo Neruda's *Canto General*

1951 Libya independent of Italy
1951 King Abdullah of Transjordan assassinated

AMERICA	ABROAD

1952 End of US occupation of Japan
1952 Ralph Ellison's *Invisible Man*
1952 Puerto Rico becomes a US Commonwealth
1952 Dwight D. Eisenhower elected president
1952 *High Noon; Singin' in the Rain*
1952 US explodes first hydrogen bomb
1953 Truce in Korea
1953 Julius and Ethel Rosenberg executed for espionage
1953 *Playboy* launched

1952 Slavery abolished in Qatar
1952 Death of Eva Peron, Argentina
1952 Mau-Mau Rebellion, Kenya
1952 First British nuclear test

1953 US and UK aid coup in Iran
1953 Crick and Watson discover structure of DNA
1953 USSR explodes its first hydrogen bomb
1953 Edmund Hillary and Tenzing Norgay summit Mount Everest
1953 East Berlin workers' uprising
1953 Stalin dies; Khruschev takes power in USSR
1953 Queen Elizabeth II crowned

1954 *Brown v. Board of Education* rules educational segregation unconstitutional:

1954 US-backed coup in Guatemala

"Separate educational facilities are inherently unequal."
CHIEF JUSTICE EARL WARREN

1954 Army-McCarthy hearings; McCarthy censured by Senate for dishonorable conduct:

1954–62 Algerian War of Independence from France

"Have you no sense of decency, sir?
At long last, have you left no sense of decency?"
JOSEPH WELCH, SPECIAL COUNSEL FOR US ARMY

1955 Rosa Parks inspires Montgomery Bus Boycott
1955 Jonas Salk develops polio vaccine
1956 Elvis Presley releases "Heartbreak Hotel"
1956 Interstate Highway Act

1954 Dien Bien Phu: French driven from Indochina by Ho Chi Minh
1956 Hungarian uprising crushed by Soviet invasion; West looks on
1956 Khruschev threatens West: "We will bury you"
1956 Suez crisis: France, Britain, and Israel battle Egypt after Nasser closes canal; forced to stand down by US

AMERICA	**ABROAD**
1957 Brooklyn Dodgers move to Los Angeles	*1957* Soviets launch Sputnik, first manmade satellite, into space
1957 Little Rock Central High School desegregation crisis	
1957 Sondheim and Bernstein's *West Side Story* on Broadway	
1958 US marines to Beirut in first Lebanese civil war	*1958–60* Mao Zedong's "Great Leap Forward" causes famine killing at least 20 million
1958 NASA established; *Explorer 1* satellite launched	
1959 Miles Davis's *Kind of Blue*	*1959* Fidel Castro overthrows Batista regime in Cuba
1959 Frank Lloyd Wright's Guggenheim Museum	*1959* Dalai Lama flees Chinese-occupied Tibet
1959 Mailer's *Advertisements for Myself*	*1960* Sino-Soviet split
1960 U-2 incident: US spy plane shot down over USSR	*1960* Nigeria independent of Britain
1960 First televised presidential debate; John F. Kennedy vs. Richard M. Nixon	*1960* Brasília completed; replaces Rio de Janeiro as capital of Brazil
1960 Sit-ins against Jim Crow laws	*1960* Sharpeville Massacre, South Africa
	1960 Israelis capture Adolf Eichmann in Argentina
	1960 Congo independence; civil war
1961 Pres. John F. Kennedy takes office:	*1961* Yuri Gagarin becomes first man in space

"My fellow Americans, ask not what your country can do for you,
ask what you can do for your country. My fellow citizens of the world,
ask not what America will do for you, but what together
we can do for the freedom of man."
INAUGURAL ADDRESS

1961 US sends aid and military advisors to South Vietnam	*1961* French army putsch against Charles de Gaulle in Algeria
1961 Peace Corps established	*1961* Berlin Crisis brings world close to war
1961 Joseph Heller's *Catch 22*	
1961 Bay of Pigs debacle, Cuba	
1962 Cuban Missile Crisis:	

"We were eyeball to eyeball and the other fellow just blinked."
SECRETARY OF STATE DEAN RUSK

1962 Federal troops enforce right of black USAF veteran James Meredith to attend "Ole Miss"	*1962* Vatican II council in Rome reforms Catholic doctrine, ritual
1963 Alabama civil rights crises; Medgar Evars murdered	*1962* War between India and China
1963 Dr. Martin Luther King, Jr.'s "Letter from a Birmingham Jail":	*1962* Leftist military coup in Burma
	1963 UN troops crush Katanga secession in Congo
	1963 Kenya independent from Britain

"Injustice anywhere is a threat to justice everywhere."

1963 King addresses crowd at March on Washington:	*1963* US-backed coup in South Vietnam; Diem assassinated

"I have a dream that my four little children will one day live in a nation where they will not be judged by the color of their skin but by the content of their character."

1963 Betty Friedan's *The Feminine Mystique* inspires feminist movement	*1963* Test Ban Treaty
1963 Assassination of Pres. John F. Kennedy, November 22, Dallas	*1963* De Gaulle refuses British EEC entry
1963 Cassius Clay defeats Sonny Liston, becomes Muhammad Ali:	

"Float like a butterfly, sting like a bee."

1964 Civil Rights Act desegregates public accommodation	*1964* Leonid Brezhnev takes power in USSR
1964 Gulf of Tonkin incident	
1964 Barry Goldwater GOP presidential candidate:	

"I would remind you that extremism in the defense of liberty is no vice!
...[And] moderation in the pursuit of justice is no virtue!"
GOLDWATER ON ACCEPTING NOMINATION

1964 Pres. Lyndon B. Johnson inaugurates "Great Society" programs:

"This administration, today, here and now declares unconditional war on poverty in America."

1964 Beatles come to America

1965 Civil Rights marchers in Selma, Alabama, attacked by police	**1965** White Rhodesian regime declares independence from Britain
1965 Voting Rights Act:	

"I have not the slightest doubt that good men from everywhere in this country, from the Great Lakes to the Gulf of Mexico...will rally now together in this cause to vindicate the freedom of all Americans."
LBJ

1965 Watts riots, Los Angeles:

"Burn, baby, burn!"
RIOTERS' SLOGAN

1965 *Griswold v. Connecticut,* Supreme Court privacy ruling overturns contraception law	**1965–71** Freedom Flights airlift refugees from Castro's Cuba to US
1965 Marines sent to civil war–torn Dominican Republic	**1965** Singapore independent of Malaysia
1965 LBJ sends first US combat units to South Vietnam	**1965** First space walk, USSR
	1965 "Year of Living Dangerously" coup in Indonesia
	1965 Second Indo-Pakistani war
	1965 Mobutu coup in Congo
1966 *Miranda v. Arizona* establishes "right to remain silent"	**1966–76** Cultural Revolution begins in China; millions die
1966 Edward W. Brooke of Massachusetts, first popularly elected black senator	
1967 Anti-war march on Pentagon	**1967** Greek Colonels' coup d'état
1967 "Summer of Love," San Francisco	**1967** First heart transplant, Cape Town, South Africa
1967 Thurgood Marshall first black appointed to Supreme Court	**1967** Che Guevara killed in Bolivia
	1967 Six Day War between Arab countries and Israel
1968 Chicago police riot at Democratic National Convention	**1968** "Prague Spring" uprising and Soviet invasion of Czechoslovakia
1968 Arthur Ashe wins first US Open at Forest Hills	**1968** Student riots in Paris; De Gaulle reelected
1968 Dr. Martin Luther King, Jr. assassinated; race riots across America	**1968** Student riots in Berlin, Tokyo, Rome, Caracas, London, Cambridge
1968 Sen. Robert F. Kennedy assassinated	**1968** Tlatelolco Massacre, Mexico City
	1968 Warsaw anti-Soviet riots

1968 Vietnamese Communist Tet Offensive collapses, but US confidence still shaken **1968** My Lai Massacre **1969** *Apollo 11*; Americans land on moon:	**1968** Baathists seize power in Iraq **1968–77** Baader-Meinhof terrorist campaign in Germany

"That's one small step for [a] man; one giant leap for mankind."
NEIL ARMSTRONG

1969 Philip Roth's *Portnoy's Complaint* **1969** "Days of Rage"; trial of "Chicago Seven"; start of Weatherman terrorism **1969** Stonewall Riots, New York, inspire Gay Liberation movement **1969** Woodstock festival **1970** Vietnam war spreads to Cambodia **1970** Kent State shootings	**1969** Soccer War between El Salvador and Honduras **1969** Troubles begin, Northern Ireland **1969** Russia-China border clashes **1970** Solzhenitsyn wins Nobel Prize **1970** Biafran revolt crushed by Nigeria **1970** Beatles break up **1970** Cyclone and tidal wave kills 500,000 in East Pakistan
1971 26th Amendment gives 18-year-olds the vote **1972** Francis Ford Coppola's *The Godfather* **1972** Nixon visits, begins détente with Red China **1972** Swimmer Mark Spitz first athlete to win seven gold medals **1973** *Roe v. Wade* establishes constitutional right to abortion **1973** US forces withdrawn from Vietnam; Paris Peace Accords end US role in war	**1971** Third India-Pakistan war; East Pakistan independent as Bangladesh **1972** PLO terrorists murder Israeli athletes at Munich Olympics **1972** 150,000 Hutus massacred, Burundi **1972** Idi Amin's Uganda expels 80,000 South Asians **1973** Yom Kippur War; Israel defeats Egyptian, Syrian attacks **1973** US-backed coup in Chile leads to Pinochet dictatorship **1973** Britain joins EEC **1973–74** OPEC global oil crisis
1974 Nixon resigns over Watergate scandal and cover-up **1974** Pres. Gerald Ford pardons Nixon, grants amnesty to draft dodgers	**1974** Ethiopia's Haile Selassie overthrown by Derg junta **1974** Solzhenitsyn's *The Gulag Archipelago*

AMERICA	ABROAD
1975 Bill Gates and Paul Allen found Microsoft **1975** Jimmy Hoffa disappears **1975** SLA kidnaps Patty Hearst **1975** Marines rescue *Mayaguez* crew **1975** *Jaws* first summer blockbluster	**1975** Saigon falls; millions of South Vietnamese sent to reeducation camps **1975** Lebanese Civil war begins **1975** Franco dies; Spain a monarchy **1975** Indonesia invades East Timor **1975** Angola independent from Portugal; civil war **1975** Laos falls to Communists **1975–77** Indira Gandhi's State of Emergency; suspension of democracy **1975–79** Cambodian Genocide; Khmer Rouge, under Pol Pot, kills 1.7 million
1976 US Bicentennial **1976** Saul Bellow wins Nobel Prize for Literature and Pulitzer Prize for Fiction **1976** *Viking 1* lands on Mars	**1976–79** One million Vietnamese "boat people" flee communist regime **1976** Israeli commandos rescue hijack hostages at Entebbe **1976** Death of Mao Zedong **1976–83** Argentina's "Dirty War" **1976** Concorde jet enters service **1976** Earthquake kills 655,000, China **1976–2005** Syrians occupy Lebanon
1977 Alex Haley's *Roots* shown on TV **1977** George Lucas's *Star Wars*	**1977** France subsidizes coronation of cannibal "Emperor" Bokassa, Central Africa **1977** General Zia's coup against Pres. Bhutto, Pakistan
1978 US-brokered Camp David Accords between Egypt and Israel **1978** Torrijos-Carter Treaty to hand over Panama Canal	**1978** Aldo Moro, Italian politician, kidnapped, killed by Red Brigades **1978** Deng Xiaoping takes power in China **1978** Jonestown, Guyana, mass-suicide
1979 First rap chart hit: "Rappers Delight" by Sugar Hill Gang **1979** US embassy in Tehran seized, 52 hostages held for 444 days **1979** President Jimmy Carter's "malaise" speech describes national loss of confidence	**1979** "Sandinista" rebels overthrow Somoza regime in Nicaragua; battle US-supported Contras **1979** Shah of Iran overthrown; Ayatollah Khomeini takes power **1979** Saddam Hussein takes power in Iraq **1979** Soviet invasion of Afghanistan **1979** Vietnam overthrows Khmer Rouge, defeats Chinese invasion

1979–90 Margaret Thatcher, British prime minister

1980 Ronald Reagan elected president
1980 US Hockey team beats USSR in Olympic "Miracle on Ice"
1980 Failed "Desert One" attempt to rescue Iran hostages

1980 Tito dies in Yugoslavia
1980–88 Saddam Hussein starts Iran-Iraq war
1980 Rhodesia attains majority rule, becomes Zimbabwe
1980–92 Civil war in El Salvador
1980 Solidarity Movement launched in Poland; martial law

1981 Reagan assassination attempt
1981 Sandra Day O'Connor first female appointed to Supreme Court
1981 John Updike's *Rabbit is Rich* wins Pulitzer Prize for Fiction
1982 Vietnam Memorial Wall erected
1982 US sends troops to Beirut
1982 AIDS identified and named

1981 Anwar Sadat assassinated, Egypt
1981 Israeli Air Force destroys Iraqi nuclear reactor

1982 Falklands war between Argentina and Britain
1982 Israel battles PLO, Syrians in Lebanon
1982 Fall of Argentine military junta after defeat
1982 Hama Massacre in Syria
1982–85 Mass murder of Matabele tribe by Robert Mugabe's army, Zimbabwe

1983 Reagan calls USSR "Evil Empire"
1983 US troops pulled out of Beirut after suicide bomb attacks; triumph of Hezbollah
1983 US intervention in Grenada
1983 *Pioneer 10* leaves solar system
1984 Apple launches Macintosh computer

1983 Sri Lankan ethnic riots lead to civil war, terrorism

1984 Indian troops storm Sikhs' Golden Temple; Indira Gandi assassinated in return
1984–85 Ethiopian famine
1985 Mexico City Earthquake
1985 Mikhail Gorbachev becomes leader of USSR
1985 French agents bomb Greenpeace ship *Rainbow Warrior*
1985 Cruise ship *Achille Lauro* hijacked by Palestinian terrorists

1986 *Challenger* Space Shuttle disaster: |

"We will never forget them, nor the last time we saw them,
this morning, as they prepared for their journey and waved goodbye and
'slipped the surly bonds of Earth' to 'touch the face of God.'"
PRES. RONALD REAGAN

1986 Greg LeMond first American to
win Tour de France
1986 Iran-Contra scandal surfaces

1986 Chernobyl nuclear accident,
Ukraine; millions affected
1986 "People power" drives dictator
Ferdinand Marcos from Manila
1986 Olof Palme, Swedish prime
minister, assassinated

The End of the Cold War: Liberty and Disorder

1987 Reagan challenges Soviets to
open communist empire:

1987 Taiwan ends martial law,
begins democracy

"Mr. Gorbachev, open this gate! Mr. Gorbachev, tear down this wall!"
REAGAN AT BERLIN'S BRANDENBERG GATE

1987 Stock market crash

1988 Pan Am Flight 103 blown up by
Libyan terrorist bomb over Lockerbie,
Scotland, killing 270

1989 US invades Panama to overthrow
drug-dealer/dictator Manuel Noriega

1989 *Exxon Valdez* oil spill

1987 South Korea holds first
democratic election
1987–90 Indian troops intervene in
Sri Lankan civil war
1988 Soviets begin pullout from
Afghanistan
1988 Saddam's Anfal campaign to
exterminate Iraq's Kurds
1989 Tiananmen Square democracy
movement crushed by Chinese army
1989 "Velvet Revolutions" overthrow
communism in Czechoslovakia,
Poland, etc.
1989 Berlin Wall comes down
1989 Ceauşescu communist regime
overthrown in Romania
1989 Dalai Lama wins Nobel
Peace Prize
1989 Ayatollah Khomenei issues fatwa
calling for murder of Salman Rushdie

1990 Pres. George Bush and Mikhail Gorbachev sign chemical weapons treaty

1990 Cease-fire, election in Nicaragua; Sandinistas lose vote, Contras disband
1990 Nelson Mandela released from prison
1990 Iraq invades and occupies Kuwait

1991 Maastricht Treaty moves EU closer to single state
1991 USSR dissolved; Boris Yeltsin, Russia's first elected leader, defeats coup
1991 Indian prime minister Rajiv Gandhi assassinated by Tamil terrorist
1991 US and Coalition forces to Saudi Arabia:

1991–94 Ethnic warfare in newly independent Caucasus states

"[It will be] the Mother of all battles."
SADDAM HUSSEIN, IRAQI DICTATOR

1991 Operation Desert Storm (First Gulf War); Kuwait liberated:

"Our strategy in going after this army is very, very simple. First we are going to cut it off, then we are going to kill it."
GEN. COLIN POWELL, CHAIRMAN OF JOINT CHIEFS

1991–2003 NATO patrolled no-fly zone established over Kurdistan, Northern Iraq
1992 Rodney King riots in Los Angeles:

1991 Tim Berners Lee invents World Wide Web

1992–95 Bosnia War in former Yugoslavia; ethnic cleansing

"Can we all get along?"
RODNEY KING

1993 Somalia intervention; "Black Hawk Down" battle in Mogadishu
1993 NAFTA free trade agreement with Mexico, Canada
1993 Islamic extremists carry out first terrorist attack on World Trade Center
1993 Siege and assault on Branch Davidian Cult at Waco, Texas

1993 Eritrea wins independence from Ethiopia

AMERICA	ABROAD
1994 US-led multinational force in Haiti	**1994** Apartheid ends in South Africa, Nelson Mandela elected President **1994** Rwanda Genocide; more than 900,000 slaughtered by French-backed Hutu regime **1994** Chiapas Rebellion, Mexico **1994** North Korean dictator Kim Il Sung dies, succeeded by son Kim Jong-Il **1994–96** First Chechen war; Russians humiliated by rebels
1995 USAF, NATO bomb Serbia to stop ethnic cleansing of Bosnian Muslims; Dayton Peace Agreement **1995** Normalization of relations with Vietnam **1995** Oklahoma City bombing **1996** Khobar towers, USAF barracks in Saudi Arabia attacked by al Qaeda terrorists	**1995** Srebrenica Massacre, Bosnia, Dutch UN peacekeepers look on **1995** Sarin gas attack on Tokyo subway
	1997 Britain surrenders Hong Kong to Communist China **1997** Tony Blair becomes British prime minister **1997** Death of Princess Diana
1998 Steven Spielberg's *Saving Private Ryan* **1998** CNN apologizes for "Tailwind" libel of Vietnam-era Green Berets **1998** Al Qaeda bombings of US Embassies in Kenya, Tanzania **1998** Starr Report and impeachment trial of Bill Clinton **1999** US forces to Kosovo to stop anti-Muslim ethnic cleansing	**1998** Good Friday Agreement, Northern Ireland **1998** Indian and Pakistani nuclear tests
	1999 Australian-led intervention in East Timor after Indonesian pogrom **1999** Gen. Pervez Musharraf's coup in Pakistan **1999** Vladimir Putin, former KGB officer, succeeds Yeltsin as Russia's president **1999** Second Chechen war begins; Russians flatten Grozny
2000 NY Yankees win a record 26th World Series	**2000** Second Intifada in Israel and Palestinian territories

2000 Al Qaeda attacks USS *Cole* off Aden **2000** Disputed presidential election; Supreme Court declares George W. Bush president	**2000** PRI regime defeated in Mexican election

Terror and Liberation

2001 Colin Powell becomes first black Secretary of State **2001** China forces down US surveillance plane **2001** 9/11: Al Qaeda terrorists fly hijacked airliners into World Trade Center, Pentagon; fourth plane crashes in Shanksville, PA:	**2001** Afghan Taliban destroys Bamiyan Buddhas **2001** Nepalese Royal Family massacre **2001** Earthquake kills 11,000 in Gujarat, India **2001** Terrorist bomb attacks on Sbarro pizzeria, Dolphinarium nightclub, Tel Aviv, Israel

"Are you guys ready? Let's roll."
TODD BEAMER, PASSENGER ON FLIGHT 93,
RALLYING OTHERS TO OVERCOME HIJACKERS

"The city is going to survive."
NEW YORK MAYOR RUDY GIULIANI

"Great tragedy has come to us, and we are meeting it with the best
that is in our country, with courage and concern for others,
because this is America. This is who we are."
PRES. GEORGE W. BUSH

2001 US declares "War on Terror" **2001** US-led coalition overthrows Taliban Islamist regime in Afghanistan, searches for Osama bin Laden	

2002 Bush speech to graduating West Point cadets outlines "preemption," pro-democracy doctrines:	**2002** British intervention in Sierra Leone civil war

"In defending the peace, we face a threat with no precedent.
If we wait for threats to fully materialize, we will have waited too long...
Our nation's cause has always been larger than our nation's defense."

2003 US peacekeepers to Liberia
2003 US-led coalition liberates Iraq
from Saddam Hussein dictatorship
2003–5 Coalition forces battle Sunni
insurgents, Shia militias, foreign
terrorists in Iraq
2004 Lance Armstrong becomes first
six-time winner of Tour de France
2004 Boston Red Sox break curse,
win World Series

2002 Moscow Theater Siege by
Chechen Islamist terrorists
2002 Al Qaeda bombs tourist
nightclubs in Bali
2002 Gujarat pogrom, India
2003–5 Darfur massacres in Sudan
2003 SARS outbreak in China
2003 Rose Revolution in Republic
of Georgia

2004 Beslan hostages massacred in
Russia by Chechen terrorists
2004 First democratic election
in Afghanistan
2004 Orange Revolution in Ukraine
2004 Tsunami devastates areas of
Southeast Asia; over 200,000 die
2004 Libya gives up nuclear weapons
program
2004 Corruption of UN Iraq
Oil-for-Food Program exposed
2004 Seven former Eastern bloc
countries join NATO
2004 Dutch filmmaker Theo van Gogh
murdered by Islamic extremists
2005 First democratic election held in
Iraq; democratic agitation throughout
Middle East
2005 Pope John Paul II dies; succeeded
by Benedict XVI

PART TWO

Patriotic Texts
& Essentials

Speeches, Charters
& Significant Documents

THE MAGNA CARTA

1215

**The Great Charter of liberties was extorted from
King John by the barons of England.**

Clause 39: No free man shall be taken or imprisoned or dispossessed, or outlawed or exiled or in any way destroyed, nor will we go upon him, nor will we send against him except by the lawful judgement of his peers or by the law of the land.

Clause 40: To no man will we sell, or deny, or delay, right or justice.

THE MAYFLOWER COMPACT

November 11, 1620

The first self-governing document of the Plymouth Colony, it was drafted on board the *Mayflower* and signed in what is now Provincetown Harbor.

In the name of God, Amen. We, whose names are underwritten, the loyal subjects of our dread sovereign Lord King James, by the grace of God, of Great Britain, France, and Ireland, king, defender of the faith, etc.

Having undertaken, for the glory of God, and advancement of the Christian faith, and honor of our king and country, a voyage to plant the first colony in the Northern parts of Virginia, do, by these presents, solemnly and mutually in the presence of God, and one of another, covenant and combine ourselves together into a civil body politic, for our better ordering and preservation and furtherance of the ends aforesaid; and by virtue hereof to enact, constitute and frame such just and equal laws, ordinances, acts, constitutions and offices, from time to time, as shall be thought most meet and convenient for the general good of the Colony unto which we promise all due submission and obedience.

In witness whereof we have hereunder subscribed our names at Cape Cod the 11th of November, in the year of the reign of our sovereign Lord King James, of England, France and Ireland the eighteenth, and of Scotland the fifty-fourth. *Anno Domini 1620*

A CITY ON A HILL

John Winthrop — *1630*

The notion that the American community is divinely ordained and destined to be a model for the world begins with this passage from the sermon "A Model of Christian Charity," delivered by the Puritan leader and future Governor of the Massachusetts Bay Colony while sailing to the New World on the ship *Arbella*. It echoes the Sermon on the Mount in Matthew's Gospel, and has inspired countless American political speeches.

We must be knit together, in this work, as one man. We must entertain each other in brotherly affection. We must be willing to abridge ourselves of our superfluities for the supply of others' necessities. We must uphold a familiar commerce together in all meekness, gentleness, patience, and liberality. We must delight in each other; make others' conditions our own; rejoice together, mourn together, labor and suffer together, always having before our eyes our commission and community in the work...that men shall say of succeeding plantations, "may the Lord make it like that of New England." For we must consider that we shall be as a city upon a hill. The eyes of all people are upon us.

THE AMERICAN CRISIS

Tom Paine — *December 25, 1776*

Written after the loss of New York on December 23, 1776, it was read to the troops on Christmas morning by order of George Washington.

THESE are the times that try men's souls. The summer soldier and the sunshine patriot will, in this crisis, shrink from the service of their country; but he that stands by it now, deserves the love and thanks of man and woman. Tyranny, like hell, is not easily conquered; yet we have this consolation with us, that the harder the conflict, the more glorious the triumph. What we obtain too cheap, we esteem too lightly: it is dearness only that gives every thing its value. Heaven knows how to put a proper price upon its goods; and it would be strange indeed if so celestial an article as FREEDOM should not be highly rated.

THE DECLARATION OF INDEPENDENCE
(Excerpted)

1776

One of the most important documents in human history, the Declaration
of Independence was drafted by John Adams of Massachussetts,
Benjamin Franklin of Pennsylvania, Thomas Jefferson of Virginia,
Robert R. Livingstone of New York, and Roger Sherman of New York.
With startling brevity and power, especially for a document created by
a committee, it succinctly expresses the principles shared by the
Founding Fathers, drawing heavily on the writings of British political
philosopher John Locke. It was adopted by the Continental Congress in
amended form on July 4, 1776, at the Pennsylvania State House.

When, in the course of human events, it becomes necessary for one people to dissolve the political bands which have connected them with another, and to assume, among the powers of the earth, the separate and equal station to which the laws of nature and of nature's God entitle them, a decent respect to the opinions of mankind requires that they should declare the causes which impel them to the separation.

We hold these truths to be self-evident:

That all men are created equal; that they are endowed by their Creator with certain unalienable rights; that among these are life, liberty, and the pursuit of happiness; that, to secure these rights, governments are instituted among men, deriving their just powers from the consent of the governed; that whenever any form of government becomes destructive of these ends, it is the right of the people to alter or to abolish it, and to institute new government, laying its foundation on such principles, and organizing its powers in such form, as to them shall seem most likely to effect their safety and happiness. Prudence, indeed, will dictate that governments long established should not be changed for light and transient causes; and accordingly all experience hath shown that mankind are more disposed to suffer, while evils are sufferable than to right themselves by abolishing the forms to which they are accustomed. But when a long train of abuses and usurpations, pursuing invariably the same object, evinces a design to reduce them under absolute despotism, it is their right, it is their duty, to throw off such government, and to provide new guards for their future security.... —Such has been the patient sufferance of these Colonies; and such is now the necessity which constrains them to alter their former Systems of Government. The history of the present King of Great Britain is a history of repeated injuries and usurpations, all having in direct object the establishment of an absolute Tyranny over these States. To prove this, let Facts be submitted to a candid world.

We, therefore, the representatives of the United States of America, in General Congress assembled, appealing to the Supreme Judge of the world for the rectitude of our intentions, do, in the name and by the authority of the good people of these colonies, solemnly publish and declare, that these United Colonies are, and of right ought to be, FREE AND INDEPENDENT STATES; that they are absolved from all allegiance to the British crown, and that all political connection between them and the state of Great Britain is, and ought to be, totally dissolved; and that, as free and independent states, they have full power to levy war, conclude peace, contract alliances, establish commerce, and do all other acts and things which independent states may of right do. And for the support of this declaration, with a firm reliance on the protection of Divine Providence, we mutually pledge to each other our lives, our fortunes, and our sacred honor.

THE PREAMBLE TO THE UNITED STATES CONSTITUTION AND THE BILL OF RIGHTS

1787–88

The "supreme law of the land," the United States Constitution was adopted by the Constitutional Convention in 1787 and took effect in 1789 after fierce battles over its ratification by the states. It is the oldest written constitution in force anywhere in the world. Unlike many of its imitators, it has survived vast social and economic changes thanks to the profound loyalty it has inspired in successive generations. Like the Declaration of Independence, its prose is deathless—its opening sentence echoes down the years and around the globe—but many men and women have given their lives to preserve it.

The Constitution has 27 amendments. The first ten, proposed in 1789 and ratified in 1791, are known as the Bill of Rights. The 14th Amendment of 1868 extended much of the Bill of Rights to the States. More than 10,000 Constitutional amendments have been proposed in Congress since 1789. The 18th Amendment, concerning the prohibition of alcohol, is the only amendment to be directly repealed by another (the 21st).

The Preamble

We the People of the United States, in Order to form a more perfect Union, establish Justice, insure domestic Tranquility, provide for the common defence, promote the general Welfare, and secure the Blessings of Liberty to ourselves and our Posterity, do ordain and establish this Constitution for the United States of America.

The Bill of Rights

Amendment I

Congress shall make no law respecting an establishment of religion, or prohibiting the free exercise thereof; or abridging the freedom of speech, or of the press; or the right of the people peaceably to assemble, and to petition the Government for a redress of grievances.

Amendment II

A well regulated Militia, being necessary to the security of a free State, the right of the people to keep and bear Arms, shall not be infringed.

Amendment III

No Soldier shall, in time of peace be quartered in any house, without the consent of the Owner, nor in time of war, but in a manner to be prescribed by law.

Amendment IV

The right of the people to be secure in their persons, houses, papers, and effects, against unreasonable searches and seizures, shall not be violated, and no Warrants shall issue, but upon probable cause, supported by Oath or affirmation, and particularly describing the place to be searched, and the persons or things to be seized.

Amendment V

No person shall be held to answer for a capital, or otherwise infamous crime, unless on a presentment or indictment of a Grand Jury, except in cases arising in the land or naval forces, or in the Militia, when in actual service in time of War or public danger; nor shall any person be subject for the same offence to be twice put in jeopardy of life or limb; nor shall be compelled in any criminal case to be a witness against himself, nor be deprived of life, liberty, or property, without due process of law; nor shall private property be taken for public use, without just compensation.

Amendment VI

In all criminal prosecutions, the accused shall enjoy the right to a speedy and public trial, by an impartial jury of the State and district wherein the crime shall have been committed, which district shall have been previously ascertained by law, and to be informed of the nature and cause of the accusation; to be confronted with the witnesses against him; to have compulsory process for obtaining witnesses in his favor, and to have the Assistance of Counsel for his defence.

Amendment VII

In Suits at common law, where the value in controversy shall exceed twenty dollars, the right of trial by jury shall be preserved, and no fact tried by a jury, shall be otherwise re-examined in any Court of the United States, than according to the rules of the common law.

Amendment VIII

Excessive bail shall not be required, nor excessive fines imposed, nor cruel and unusual punishments inflicted.

Amendment IX

The enumeration in the Constitution, of certain rights, shall not be construed to deny or disparage others retained by the people.

Amendment X

The powers not delegated to the United States by the Constitution, nor prohibited by it to the States, are reserved to the States respectively, or to the people.

TO BIGOTRY NO SANCTION

George Washington ~ *August 19, 1790*

The new president's letter to the Hebrew Congregation of Newport, RI, eloquently expresses his belief in America as a beacon of liberty.

The citizens of the United States of America have a right to applaud themselves for having given to mankind examples of an enlarged and liberal policy—a policy worthy of imitation... It is now no more that toleration is spoken of as if it were the indulgence of one class of people that another enjoyed the exercise of their inherent natural rights, for, happily, the Government of the United States, which gives to bigotry no sanction, to persecution no assistance, requires only that they who live under its protection should demean themselves as good citizens in giving it on all occasions their effectual support.

May the children of the stock of Abraham who dwell in this land continue to merit and enjoy the good will of the other inhabitants—while every one shall sit in safety under his own vine and fig tree and there shall be none to make him afraid.

THE GETTYSBURG ADDRESS [entire]

Abraham Lincoln ~ *November 19, 1863*

Perhaps the greatest American speech of all, it was delivered at the dedication of the Soldiers' National Cemetery four months after the Civil War's biggest battle.

Four score and seven years ago our fathers brought forth on this continent, a new nation, conceived in Liberty, and dedicated to the proposition that all men are created equal.

Now we are engaged in a great civil war, testing whether that nation, or any nation so conceived and so dedicated, can long endure. We are met on a great battlefield of that war. We have come to dedicate a portion of that field as a final resting place for those who here gave their lives that the nation might live. It is altogether fitting and proper, that we should do this.

But, in a larger sense, we cannot dedicate—we cannot consecrate—we cannot hallow—this ground. The brave men, living and dead, who struggled here, have consecrated it, far above our poor power to add or detract. The world will little note, nor long remember what we say here, but it can never forget what they did here. It is for us the living, rather, to be dedicated here to the unfinished work which they who fought here have thus far so nobly advanced. It is rather for us to be here dedicated to the great task remaining before us—that from these honored dead we take increased devotion to that cause for which they gave the last full measure of devotion—that we here highly resolve that these dead shall not have died in vain—that this nation, under God, shall have a new birth of freedom—and that government of the people, by the people, for the people, shall not perish from the earth.

LINCOLN'S SECOND INAUGURAL ADDRESS

Abraham Lincoln ⟶ *March 4, 1865*

Lincoln's own favorite, this extraordinary speech is best known for the phrase "with malice towards none," though it is shot through with a sense that the bloodshed of the Civil War was God's inevitable punishment for the evil of slavery.

The Almighty has His own purposes. "Woe unto the world because of offenses; for it must needs be that offenses come; but woe to that man by whom the offense cometh." If we shall suppose that American slavery is one of those offenses which, in the providence of God, must needs come, but which, having continued through His appointed time, He now wills to remove, and that He gives to both North and South this terrible war as the woe due to those by whom the offense came, shall we discern therein any departure from those divine attributes which the believers in a living God always ascribe to Him? Fondly do we hope, fervently do we pray, that this mighty scourge of war may speedily pass away. Yet, if God wills that it continue until all the wealth piled by the bondsman's two hundred and fifty years of unrequited toil shall be sunk, and until every drop of blood drawn by the lash shall be paid by another drawn with the sword, as was said three thousand years ago, so still it must be said, "The judgments of the Lord are true and righteous altogether."

With malice toward none, with charity for all, with firmness in the right, as God gives us to see the right, let us strive on to finish the work we are in, to bind up the nation's wounds, to care for him who shall have borne the battle and for his widow and his orphan, to do all which may achieve and cherish a just and lasting peace among ourselves and with all nations.

WILSON'S "SAFE FOR DEMOCRACY" SPEECH

Woodrow Wilson ⟶ *April 2, 1917*

Woodrow Wilson's great speech to Congress seeking a declaration of war against Imperial Germany was anchored in American idealism. It heralded the beginning of American global engagement.

The world must be made safe for democracy.... It is a fearful thing to lead this great peaceful people into war, into the most terrible and disastrous of all wars, civilization itself seeming to be in the balance. But the right is more precious than peace, and we shall fight for the things which we have always carried nearest our hearts—for democracy...for the rights and liberties of small nations, for a universal dominion of right by such a concert of free peoples as shall bring peace and safety to all nations and make the world itself at last free.

THE FOUR FREEDOMS

Franklin Delano Roosevelt — *January 6, 1941*

Part of the President's inaugural address to Congress, and written at a time
when war clouds were clearly on the horizon, this excerpt expressed his
idealistic vision of the future (and inspired four Norman Rockwell paintings
reproduced as postage stamps).

As men do not live by bread alone, they do not fight by armaments alone. Those who
man our defenses and those behind them who build our defenses must have the
stamina and the courage which come from an unshakable belief in the manner of life
which they are defending. The mighty action that we are calling for cannot be based
on a disregard of all the things worth fighting for. . . .

In the future days, which we seek to make secure, we look forward to a world
founded upon four essential human freedoms.

The first is freedom of speech and expression—everywhere in the world.

The second is freedom of every person to worship God in his own way—
everywhere in the world.

The third is freedom from want, which, translated into world terms, means
economic understandings which will secure to every nation a healthy peacetime life
for its inhabitants—everywhere in the world.

The fourth is freedom from fear, which, translated into world terms, means a
world-wide reduction of armaments to such a point and in such a thorough fashion
that no nation will be in a position to commit an act of physical aggression against any
neighbor—anywhere in the world.

That is no vision of a distant millennium. It is a definite basis for a kind of world
attainable in our own time and generation. That kind of world is the very antithesis of
the so-called "new order" of tyranny which the dictators seek to create with the crash
of a bomb. . . .

This nation has placed its destiny in the hands, heads and hearts of its millions
of free men and women, and its faith in freedom under the guidance of God. Freedom
means the supremacy of human rights everywhere. Our support goes to those who
struggle to gain those rights and keep them. Our strength is our unity of purpose.

To that high concept there can be no end save victory.

LIBERTY LIES IN THE HEARTS OF MEN AND WOMEN

Judge Learned Hand — *May 21, 1944*

Often called the "tenth justice of the Supreme Court," Hand delivered this speech at "I Am an American Day" in Central Park, New York.

Liberty lies in the hearts of men and women; when it dies there, no constitution, no law, no court can even do much to help it. While it lies there it needs no constitution, no law, no court to save it. What then is the spirit of liberty? I cannot define it; I can only tell you my own faith. The spirit of liberty is the spirit which is not too sure that it is right. . . . In the spirit of that America for which our young men are at this moment fighting and dying; in that spirit of liberty and of America I ask you to rise and with me pledge our faith in the glorious destiny of our beloved country.

ADDRESS TO D-DAY FORCES [entire]

General Dwight D. Eisenhower — *June 6, 1944*

This was Ike's order of the day, delivered at the beginning of Operation Overlord, the largest seaborne invasion in history, and the beginning of the liberation of Europe from Nazi tyranny.

Soldiers, Sailors and Airmen of the Allied Expeditionary Force!

You are about to embark upon the Great Crusade, toward which we have striven these many months. The eyes of the world are upon you. The hopes and prayers of liberty-loving people everywhere march with you. In company with our brave Allies and brothers-in-arms on other Fronts, you will bring about the destruction of the German war machine, the elimination of Nazi tyranny over the oppressed peoples of Europe, and security for ourselves in a free world.

Your task will not be an easy one. Your enemy is well trained, well equipped and battle-hardened. He will fight savagely.

But this is the year 1944! Much has happened since the Nazi triumphs of 1940–41. The United States have inflicted upon the Germans great defeats, in open battle, man-to-man. Our air offensive has seriously reduced their strength in the air and their capacity to wage war on the ground. Our Home Fronts have given us an overwhelming superiority in weapons and munitions of war, and placed at our disposal great reserves of trained fighting men. The tide has turned! The free men of the world are marching together to Victory!

I have full confidence in your courage, devotion to duty and skill in battle. We will accept nothing less than full Victory!

Good Luck! And let us all beseech the blessing of Almighty God upon this great and noble undertaking.

KENNEDY'S INAUGURAL ADDRESS

John F. Kennedy — *January 20, 1961*

With its ringing summons to fight for liberty and justice around the world, this speech transcends its Cold War origins and speaks powerfully to Americans today.

Let the word go forth from this time and place, to friend and foe alike, that the torch has been passed to a new generation of Americans—born in this century, tempered by war, disciplined by a hard and bitter peace, proud of our ancient heritage, and unwilling to witness or permit the slow undoing of those human rights to which this nation has always been committed, and to which we are committed today at home and around the world.

Let every nation know, whether it wishes us well or ill, that we shall pay any price, bear any burden, meet any hardship, support any friend, oppose any foe, to assure the survival and the success of liberty.

This much we pledge—and more....

In your hands, my fellow citizens, more than in mine, will rest the final success or failure of our course. Since this country was founded, each generation of Americans has been summoned to give testimony to its national loyalty. The graves of young Americans who answered the call to service surround the globe

Now the trumpet summons us again—not as a call to bear arms, though arms we need—not as a call to battle, though embattled we are—but a call to bear the burden of a long twilight struggle, year in and year out, "rejoicing in hope; patient in tribulation" a struggle against the common enemies of man: tyranny, poverty, disease, and war itself....

In the long history of the world, only a few generations have been granted the role of defending freedom in its hour of maximum danger. I do not shrink from this responsibility—I welcome it. I do not believe that any of us would exchange places with any other people or any other generation. The energy, the faith, the devotion which we bring to this endeavor will light our country and all who serve it. And the glow from that fire can truly light the world.

And so, my fellow Americans, ask not what your country can do for you, ask what you can do for your country.

My fellow citizens of the world, ask not what America will do for you, but what together we can do for the freedom of man.

Finally, whether you are citizens of America or citizens of the world, ask of us here the same high standards of strength and sacrifice which we ask of you. With a good conscience our only sure reward, with history the final judge of our deeds, let us go forth to lead the land we love, asking His blessing and His help, but knowing that here on earth God's work must truly be our own.

I HAVE A DREAM

Dr. Martin Luther King, Jr. ⟶ *August 28, 1963*

One of the most famous speeches in history, this call for the end of all
discrimination was delivered by the civil rights leader
on the steps of the Lincoln Memorial.

Five score years ago, a great American, in whose symbolic shadow we stand signed
the Emancipation Proclamation. This momentous decree came as a great beacon light
of hope to millions of Negro slaves who had been seared in the flames of withering
injustice. It came as a joyous daybreak to end the long night of captivity. But one
hundred years later, we must face the tragic fact that the Negro is still not free.

One hundred years later, the life of the Negro is still sadly crippled by the
manacles of segregation and the chains of discrimination....

I have a dream that one day this nation will rise up and live out the true meaning
of its creed: "We hold these truths to be self-evident: that all men are created equal."

I have a dream that one day on the red hills of Georgia the sons of former slaves
and the sons of former slave owners will be able to sit down together at a table
of brotherhood.

I have a dream that one day even the state of Mississippi, a state sweltering with
the heat of injustice, sweltering with the heat of oppression, will be transformed into
an oasis of freedom and justice.

I have a dream that my four children will one day live in a nation where they will
not be judged by the color of their skin but by the content of their character.

I have a dream today....This will be the day when all of God's children will
be able to sing with a new meaning, "My country, 'tis of thee, sweet land of liberty,
of thee I sing. Land where my fathers died, land of the pilgrim's pride, from every
mountainside, let freedom ring." And if America is to be a great nation this must
become true. So let freedom ring from the prodigious hilltops of New Hampshire.
Let freedom ring from the mighty mountains of New York. Let freedom ring from
the heightening Alleghenies of Pennsylvania!

Let freedom ring from the snowcapped Rockies of Colorado!

Let freedom ring from the curvaceous slopes of California!

But not only that; let freedom ring from Stone Mountain of Georgia!

Let freedom ring from Lookout Mountain of Tennessee!

Let freedom ring from every hill and molehill of Mississippi. From every
mountainside, let freedom ring. And when this happens, When we allow freedom to
ring, when we let it ring from every village and every hamlet, from every state and every
city, we will be able to speed up that day when all of God's children, black men and
white men, Jews and Gentiles, Protestants and Catholics, will be able to join hands
and sing in the words of the old Negro spiritual, "Free at last! Free at last! Thank God
Almighty, we are free at last!"

POINTE DU HOC SPEECH

Ronald Reagan — *June 6, 1984*

Delivered by Ronald Reagan on the 40th anniversary of D-Day, near the Pointe du Hoc Memorial in Normandy, France.

We're here to mark that day in history when the Allied armies joined in battle to reclaim this continent to liberty.... Forty years ago at this moment, the air was dense with smoke and the cries of men, and the air was filled with the crack of rifle fire and the roar of cannon. At dawn, on the morning of the 6th of June, 1944, 225 Rangers jumped off the British landing craft and ran to the bottom of these cliffs. Their mission was one of the most difficult and daring of the invasion: to climb these sheer and desolate cliffs and take out the enemy guns.... Behind me is a memorial that symbolizes the Ranger daggers that were thrust into the top of these cliffs. And before me are the men who put them there. These are the boys of Pointe du Hoc. These are the men who took the cliffs. These are the champions who helped free a continent. These are the heroes who helped end a war....

Forty summers have passed since the battle that you fought here. You were young the day you took these cliffs; some of you were hardly more than boys, with the deepest joys of life before you. Yet, you risked everything here. Why?... We look at you, and somehow we know the answer. It was faith and belief; it was loyalty and love.... You all knew that some things are worth dying for. One's country is worth dying for, and democracy is worth dying for, because it's the most deeply honorable form of government ever devised by man.... let us make a vow to our dead. Let us show them by our actions that we understand what they died for. Let our actions say to them the words for which Matthew Ridgway listened: "I will not fail thee nor forsake thee."

A FORWARD POLICY OF FREEDOM

George W. Bush — *November 6, 2003*

Delivered at the 20th Anniversary of the National Endowment for Democracy in Washington, DC, this speech proclaimed a revolution in US foreign policy in favor of promoting democracy in the Middle East and around the world.

The advance of freedom is the calling of our time; it is the calling of our country. From the Fourteen Points to the Four Freedoms, to the Speech at Westminster, America has put our power at the service of principle. We believe that liberty is the design of nature; we believe that liberty is the direction of history. We believe that human fulfillment and excellence come in the responsible exercise of liberty. And we believe that freedom—the freedom we prize—is not for us alone, it is the right and the capacity of all mankind.

Songs

THE STAR-SPANGLED BANNER

Francis Scott Key — *1814*

Written at Fort McHenry, it has been the National Anthem since 1931.

O! say can you see, by the dawn's early light,
What so proudly we hailed at the twilight's last gleaming?
Whose broad stripes and bright stars, through the perilous fight,
O'er the ramparts we watched, were so gallantly streaming?
And the rocket's red glare, the bombs bursting in air,
Gave proof through the night that our flag was still there.
O! say, does that star-spangled banner yet wave
O'er the land of the free and the home of the brave?

MY COUNTRY 'TIS OF THEE

Samuel F. Smith — *1832*

This song was sung to the same tune as the national anthem of Great Britain and several British Commonwealth countries.

My country, 'tis of thee,
Sweet land of liberty—
Of thee I sing.
Land, where my fathers died;
Land of the pilgrim's pride;
From every mountainside,
Let freedom ring.

THE CONCORD HYMN [entire]

Ralph Waldo Emerson — *1836*

Sung at the completion of the Concord Monument, April 19, 1836, this poem by the great American poet, philosopher, and writer immortalizes the minutemen who sparked the American Revolution, and hints at its global impact.

By the rude bridge that arched the flood,
    Their flag to April's breeze unfurled;
Here once the embattled farmers stood;
    And fired the shot heard round the world.

The foe long since in silence slept;
    Alike the conqueror silent sleeps,
And Time the ruined bridge has swept
    Down the dark stream that seaward creeps.

On this green bank, by this soft stream,
    We place with joy a votive stone,
That memory may their deeds redeem,
    When, like our sires, our sons are gone.

O Thou who made those heroes dare
    To die, and leave their children free, —
Bid Time and Nature gently spare
    The shaft we raised to them and Thee.

BATTLE HYMN OF THE REPUBLIC

Julia Ward Howe — *1861*

Howe wrote the lyrics to music by William Steffe, which was already the foundation of the song "John Brown's Body," so popular with Union troops.

Mine eyes have seen the glory of the coming of the Lord;
He is trampling out the vintage where the grapes of wrath are stored;
He hath loosed the fateful lightning of His terrible swift sword;
His truth is marching on.

> *Chorus:*
> *Glory! Glory! Hallelujah!*
> *Glory! Glory! Hallelujah!*
> *Glory! Glory! Hallelujah!*
> *His truth is marching on.*

I have seen Him in the watchfires of a hundred circling camps,
They have builded Him an altar in the evening dews and damps;
I can read His righteous sentence by the dim and flaring lamps:
His day is marching on.

He has sounded forth the trumpet that shall never call retreat;
He is sifting out the hearts of men before His judgment seat:
Oh, be swift, my soul, to answer Him! be jubilant, my feet!
Our God is marching on.

In the beauty of the lilies Christ was born across the sea,
With a glory in His bosom that transfigures you and me:
As He died to make men holy, let us die to make men free,
While God is marching on.

THE MARINE CORPS HYMN [entire]

Anonymous — mid-19th century.

The author of the lyrics is unknown; the music is from an opera by
Jacques Offenbach. Winston Churchill, an ardent admirer of the
US Marine Corps, knew all three verses by heart.

From the halls of Montezuma
To the shores of Tripoli,
We fight our country's battles
In the air, on land, and sea.
First to fight for right and freedom,
And to keep our honor clean,
We are proud to claim the title
Of United States Marine.

Our flag's unfurl'd to every breeze
From dawn to setting sun;
We have fought in every clime and place
Where we could take a gun.
In the snow of far-off Northern lands
And in sunny tropic scenes;
You will find us always on the job—
The United States Marines.

Here's health to you and to our Corps
Which we are proud to serve;
In many a strife we've fought for life
And never lost our nerve.
If the Army and the Navy
Ever look on Heaven's scenes,
They will find the streets are guarded
By United States Marines.

HOME ON THE RANGE

Daniel E. Kelley, to music by Brewster Higley — *1870*

The state song of Kansas, its lyrics continue to capture the spirit of the West and the call of the wild.

Oh, give me a home, where the buffalo roam,
Where the deer and the antelope play,
Where seldom is heard a discouraging word,
And the skies are not cloudy all day.

Chorus:
Home, home on the range,
Where the deer and the antelope play,
Where seldom is heard a discouraging word,
And the skies are not cloudy all day.

Oh, give me a land where the bright diamond sand
Flows leisurely down the stream;
Where the graceful white swan goes gliding along
Like a maid in a heavenly dream.

The red man was pressed from this part of the West,
He's likely no more to return
To the banks of Red River where seldom if ever
Their flickering campfires burn.

Where the air is so pure, the zephyrs so free,
The breezes so balmy and light,
That I would not exchange my home on the range
For all the cities so bright.

AMERICA THE BEAUTIFUL

Katherine Lee Bates — *1893*

Bates, a schoolteacher, was inspired to write this unofficial national anthem by a trip up Pike's Peak, in Colorado.

O beautiful for spacious skies,
For amber waves of grain,
For purple mountain majesties
Above the fruited plain!
America! America!
God shed his grace on thee
And crown thy good with brotherhood
From sea to shining sea!

O beautiful for patriot dream
That sees beyond the years
Thine alabaster cities gleam
Undimmed by human tears!
America! America!
God shed his grace on thee
And crown thy good with brotherhood
From sea to shining sea!

OVER THERE

George M. Cohan — *1917*

Cohan wrote this patriotic ditty on a train days after Wilson's declaration of war. It became the most popular song of its day.

Johnnie get your gun, get your gun, get your gun,
Take it on the run, on the run, on the run,
Hear them calling you and me;
Every son of Liberty
Hurry right away, no delay, go today,
Make your daddy glad to have had such a lad
Tell your sweetheart not to pine,
To be proud her boy's in line.
Over There, Over There
Send the word, send the word, Over There
That the Yanks are coming, the Yanks are coming.

GOD BLESS AMERICA [entire]

Irving Berlin — *1918*

This unofficial national anthem was the preferred song at
memorials for the 9/11 terrorist attacks.

God Bless America,
Land that I love.
Stand beside her, and guide her
Through the night with a light from above.

From the Mountains,
To the prairies,
To the oceans white with foam.
God bless America,
My home, sweet home.

THIS LAND IS YOUR LAND

Woody Guthrie — *1940*

An "Okie" who fled the Dust Bowl during the Depression,
Guthrie was a left-wing radical, a WWII GI, a merchant seaman,
and the most famous and beloved of American folk singers.

This land is your land, this land is my land,
From California to the New York Island,
From the Redwood Forest, to the Gulf Stream waters,
This land was made for you and me

As I was walking,
That ribbon of highway,
I saw above me
That endless skyway,
I saw below me
That golden valley.
This land was made for you and me.

Poems & Verse

PAUL REVERE'S RIDE

Henry Wadsworth Longfellow — *1861*

**Silversmith Paul Revere was a Patriot propagandist before his famous ride.
He was in fact prevented from reaching Concord by a redcoat patrol,
but Longfellow's poem made Revere more famous than
Sam Prescott, his comrade who did.**

Listen my children and you shall hear
Of the midnight ride of Paul Revere,
On the eighteenth of April, in Seventy-five;
Hardly a man is now alive
Who remembers that famous day and year.

A hurry of hoofs in a village street,
A shape in the moonlight, a bulk in the dark,
And beneath from the pebbles, in passing, a spark
Struck out by a steed flying fearless and fleet;
That was all! And yet, through the gloom and the light,
The fate of a nation was riding that night;
And the spark struck out by that steed, in his flight,
Kindled the land into flame with its heat.

So through the night rode Paul Revere;
And so through the night went his cry of alarm
To every Middlesex village and farm,—
A cry of defiance, and not of fear,
A voice in the darkness, a knock at the door,
And a word that shall echo for evermore!
For, borne on the night-wind of the Past,
Through all our history, to the last,
In the hour of darkness and peril and need,
The people will waken and listen to hear
The hurrying hoof-beats of that steed,
And the midnight message of Paul Revere.

THE NEW COLOSSUS

Emma Lazarus — *1883*

Lazarus published this sonnet—inspired by the sight of refugees arriving from Russia—to raise funds for the Statue of Liberty's pedestal. These words are inscribed on its base:

"Give me your tired, your poor,
　Your huddled masses yearning to breathe free,
　The wretched refuse of your teeming shore,
　Send these, the homeless, tempest-tossed to me,
　I lift my lamp beside the golden door!"

PIONEERS! O PIONEERS!

Walt Whitman — *From Leaves of Grass, 1900*

Whitman, along with Emily Dickinson one of the two giants of American poetry, spoke with a distinctively American and democratic voice that changed the literature of the Americas forever.

COME my tan-faced children,
Follow well in order, get your weapons ready,
Have you your pistols? have you your sharp-edged axes?
Pioneers! O pioneers!

For we cannot tarry here,
We must march my darlings, we must bear the brunt of danger,
We the youthful sinewy races, all the rest on us depend,
Pioneers! O pioneers!

O you youths, Western youths,
So impatient, full of action, full of manly pride and friendship,
Plain I see you Western youths, see you tramping with the foremost,
Pioneers! O pioneers!

Have the elder races halted?
Do they droop and end their lesson, wearied over there beyond
　　the seas?
We take up the task eternal, and the burden and the lesson,
Pioneers! O pioneers!

United States Presidents

1 George Washington *1789–97*

2 John Adams *1797–1801*

3 Thomas Jefferson *1801–09*

4 James Madison *1809–17*

5 James Monroe *1817–25*

6 John Quincy Adams *1825–29*

7 Andrew Jackson *1829–37*

8 Martin Van Buren *1837–41*

9 William Henry Harrison *1841*

10 John Tyler *1841–45*

11 James K. Polk *1845–49*

12 Zachary Taylor *1849–50*

13 Millard Fillmore *1850–53*

14 Franklin Pierce *1853–57*

15 James Buchanan *1857–61*

16 Abraham Lincoln *1861–65*

17 Andrew Johnson *1865–69*

18 Ulysses S. Grant *1869–77*

19 Rutherford B. Hayes *1877–1881*

20 James A. Garfield *1881*

21 Chester A. Arthur *1881–85*

22 Grover Cleveland *1885–89*

23 Benjamin Harrison *1889–93*

24 Grover Cleveland *1893–97*

25 William McKinley *1897–1901*

26 Theodore Roosevelt *1901–09*

27 William Howard Taft *1909–13*

28 Woodrow Wilson *1913–21*

29 Warren G. Harding *1921–23*

30 Calvin Coolidge *1923–29*

31 Herbert Hoover *1929–33*

32 Franklin D. Roosevelt *1933–45*

33 Harry S Truman *1945–53*

34 Dwight D. Eisenhower *1953–61*

35 John F. Kennedy *1961–63*

36 Lyndon B. Johnson *1963–69*

37 Richard M. Nixon *1969–74*

38 Gerald Ford *1974–77*

39 Jimmy Carter *1977–81*

40 Ronald Reagan *1981–89*

41 George H.W. Bush *1989–93*

42 William J. Clinton *1993–2001*

43 George W. Bush *2001–*

The States
in Order of Joining the Union

1 Delaware *December 7, 1787*

2 Pennsylvania *December 12, 1787*

3 New Jersey *December 18, 1787*

4 Georgia *January 2, 1788*

5 Connecticut *January 9, 1788*

6 Massachusetts *February 6, 1788*

7 Maryland *April 28, 1788*

8 South Carolina *May 23, 1788*

9 New Hampshire *June 21, 1788*

10 Virginia *June 25, 1788*

11 New York *July 26, 1788*

12 North Carolina *November 21, 1789*

13 Rhode Island *May 29, 1790*

14 Vermont *March 4, 1791*

15 Kentucky *June 1, 1792*

16 Tennessee *June 1, 1796*

17 Ohio *March 1, 1803*

18 Louisiana *April 30, 1812*

19 Indiana *December 11, 1816*

20 Mississippi *December 10, 1817*

21 Illinois *December 3, 1818*

22 Alabama *December 14, 1819*

23 Maine *March 15, 1820*

24 Missouri *August 10, 1821*

25 Arkansas *June 15, 1836*

26 Michigan *January 26, 1837*

27 Florida *March 3, 1845*

28 Texas *December 29, 1845*

29 Iowa *December 28, 1846*

30 Wisconsin *May 29, 1848*

31 California *September 9, 1850*

32 Minnesota *May 11, 1858*

33 Oregon *February 14, 1859*

34 Kansas *January 29, 1861*

35 West Virginia *June 20, 1863*

36 Nevada *October 31, 1864*

37 Nebraska *March 1, 1867*

38 Colorado *August 1, 1876*

39 North Dakota *November 2, 1889*

40 South Dakota *November 2, 1889*

41 Montana *November 8, 1889*

42 Washington *November 11, 1889*

43 Idaho *July 3, 1890*

44 Wyoming *July 10, 1890*

45 Utah *January 4, 1896*

46 Oklahoma *November 16, 1907*

47 New Mexico *January 6, 1912*

48 Arizona *February 14, 1912*

49 Alaska *January 3, 1959*

50 Hawaii *August 21, 1959*

What is Patriotism?

A SELECTION OF QUOTATIONS PERTAINING TO AMERICAN PATRIOTISM

pa·tri·ot·ism *n* love for and devotion to one's country

Many things have been said and written on the subject of patriotism, some of them concerning the exploitation or abuse of patriotic feeling. Perhaps the most famous if misunderstood quotation on the subject was a throwaway remark by Dr. Samuel Johnson, the 18th-century English wit, poet, and lexicographer. It was he who said that "patriotism is the last refuge of a scoundrel." That is something that can certainly be true, though the good doctor was likely referring to the Patriotic party in the British Parliament of the time. He himself wrote an approving essay entitled "The Patriot," and defined "patriot" approvingly in his *Great Dictionary* of 1755 as "one whose ruling passion is love of his country."

Below is a selection of quotations about America and patriotism from a variety of persons who tend to see patriotic feeling as something more than mere ancestor worship or tribal identity. Some of them are famous, others are today obscure. But their words speak to what it is to be an American patriot today.

> *"Each man must for himself alone decide what is right and what is wrong, which course is patriotic and which isn't. You cannot shirk this and be a man."*
>
> MARK TWAIN

> *"The patriots are those who love America enough to see her as a model for mankind."*
>
> ADLAI STEVENSON

> *"From the very beginning our people have markedly combined practical capacity for affairs with power of devotion to an ideal. The lack of either quality would have rendered the other of small value."*
>
> THEODORE ROOSEVELT

"If the American dream is for Americans only, it will remain our dream and never be our destiny."

RENE DE VISME WILLIAMSON

"France was a land. England was a people. But America having about it still that quality of the idea, was harder to utter—it was the graves at Shiloh, and the tired, drawn, nervous faces of its great men, and the country boys dying in the Argonne for a phrase that was empty before their bodies withered. It was a willingness of the heart."

F. SCOTT FITZGERALD

"Americanism means the virtues of courage, honor, justice, truth, sincerity and hardihood—the things that made America. The things that will destroy America are prosperity at any price, peace at any price, safety first instead of duty first, the love of soft living, and the get-rich-quick theory of life."

THEODORE ROOSEVELT

"One cannot be an American by going about saying one is an American. It is necessary to feel America, like America, love America and then work."

GEORGIA O'KEEFE

"His foreparents came to America in immigrant ships. My foreparents came to America in slave ships. But whatever the original ships, we're in the same boat tonight."

REV. JESSE JACKSON

"The United States is like a gigantic boiler. Once the fire is lighted under it, there is no limit to the power it can generate."

EARL GREY, BRITISH FOREIGN MINISTER

"True patriotism springs from a belief in the dignity of the individual, freedom and equality not only for Americans but for all people on earth."

ELEANOR ROOSEVELT

"He who love not his home and his country which he has seen, how shall he love humanity in general which he has not seen?"

WILLIAM RALPH INGE

Medals for Valor

THE MEDAL OF HONOR

The Medal of Honor is the highest award for valor that the United States can bestow on members of its Armed Forces. It is presented by the president and awarded in the name of Congress. Though popularly known as the Congressional Medal of Honor, its official name is simply the "Medal of Honor." It is awarded "for conspicuous gallantry and intrepidity at the risk of life, above and beyond the call of duty, in action involving actual conflict with an opposing armed force."

Originally it was only issued to members of the US Army (and until 1891 only to enlisted men). Today the Air Force and Navy (including the Marine Corps) also issue versions of the medal with slightly altered design features.

Tradition holds that Medal of Honor winners, whatever their rank, must be saluted by all other service members, up to and including five-star generals and the Commander in Chief.

The Medal of Honor is the only military service decoration that may not be privately bought, traded, or sold.

As of this writing, a total of 3,459 Medals of Honor have been awarded since the medal was first authorized in 1862. But the criteria for its award became considerably stricter in 1916 and then again after World War II. Since then, Medals of Honor have only been awarded to military personnel engaged in action against the enemy, in cases of extreme bravery above and beyond the call of duty, and where service members put their comrades' safety before their own lives. Of the 851 Medals of Honor awarded since 1945, 525 were awarded posthumously.

Only three new Medals of Honor have been awarded since the end of the Vietnam War. None were awarded for the First Gulf War or for the operations in Grenada, Panama, and Lebanon. Two Medals were awarded, both posthumously, for the peacekeeping operation in Mogadishu, Somalia, in 1993, to Master Sergeant Gary I. Gordon and Sergeant First Class Randall D. Shughart of Task Force Ranger.

The most recent Medal of Honor was awarded (posthumously) on April 4, 2005, to Sergeant First Class Paul R. Smith, of the US Army's Third Infantry Division ("Rock of the Marne"), for his "extraordinary heroism and uncommon valor" during the fighting for Baghdad International Airport on April 4, 2003.

CONFLICTS/MEDALS OF HONOR AWARDED

Civil War	1522	Dominican Campaign	3
Indian Campaigns	426	World War I	124
1871 Korean Campaign	15	Haitian Campaign (1919–20)	2
Spanish-American War	110	Nicaraguan Campaign	2
Samoan Campaign	4	World War II	464
Philippine Insurrection	80	Korean War	131
Action Against Philippine Outlaws	6	Vietnam War	245
Boxer Rebellion	59	Action in Somalia	2
Mexican Campaign	56	Non-Combat	193
Haitian Campaign (1915)	6	Unknowns	9

Total Number of Medals of Honor Awarded by Service Branch

Army	2400
Navy	745
Marine Corps	296
Air Force	17
Coast Guard	1
Total Medals Awarded	3,459
Medals Awarded Posthumously	614

(NOTE: The civilian equivalent of the Medal of Honor is the Presidential Medal of Freedom. The equivalent of the Medal of Honor in Great Britain and in British Commonwealth countries like Australia and Canada is the Victoria Cross.)

OTHER MEDALS FOR VALOR

The second-highest medal that can be awarded to a member of the US military is the Distinguished Service Cross for soldiers, the Navy Cross for sailors and marines, and the Air Force Cross.

The third-highest medal issued for valor is the Silver Star. It is available to members of all branches of the military, and is awarded for "gallantry in action against an opposing armed force."

The Bronze Star is the fourth highest medal of valor, and is awarded for "Heroic or meritorious achievement of service not involving aerial flight in connection with operations against an Opposing armed force."

The Purple Heart or Badge of Merit (established by General George Washington on August 7, 1782, and revived in 1932) is awarded for being "wounded in action as a direct result of enemy actions."

Flag Tradition & Etiquette

"The things that the flag stands for were created by the experiences of a great people. Everything that it stands for was written by their lives."

WOODROW WILSON

"It is the flag just as much of the man who was naturalized yesterday as of the man whose people have been here for generations."

HENRY CABOT LODGE

In 1942 Congress passed a joint resolution summarizing the rules for display of the flag. The Federal Flag Code does not proscribe any behavior: it is merely a codification of customs and traditions. Here are two sections addressing respect for the flag:

FEDERAL FLAG CODE, TITLE 4, USCA

Sec. 176. Respect for flag

No disrespect should be shown to the flag of the United States of America; the flag should not be dipped to any person or thing. Regimental colors, State flags, and organization or institutional flags are to be dipped as a mark of honor.

(a) The flag should never be displayed with the union down, except as a signal of dire distress in instances of extreme danger to life or property.

(b) The flag should never touch anything beneath it, such as the ground, the floor, water, or merchandise.

(c) The flag should never be carried flat or horizontally, but always aloft and free.

(d) The flag should never be used as wearing apparel, bedding, or drapery. It should never be festooned, drawn back, nor up, in folds, but always allowed to fall free. Bunting of blue, white, and red, always arranged with the blue above, the white in the middle, and the red below, should be used for covering a speaker's desk, draping the front of the platform, and for decoration in general.

(e) The flag should never be fastened, displayed, used, or stored in such a manner as to permit it to be easily torn, soiled, or damaged in any way.

(f) The flag should never be used as a covering for a ceiling.

(g) The flag should never have placed upon it, nor on any part of it, nor attached to it any mark, insignia, letter, word, figure, design, picture, or drawing of any nature.

(h) The flag should never be used as a receptacle for receiving, holding, carrying, or delivering anything.

(i) The flag should never be used for advertising purposes in any manner whatsoever. It should not be embroidered on such articles as cushions or handkerchiefs and the like, printed or otherwise impressed on paper napkins or boxes or anything that is designed for temporary use and discard. Advertising signs should not be fastened to a staff or halyard from which the flag is flown.

(j) No part of the flag should ever be used as a costume or athletic uniform. However, a flag patch may be affixed to the uniform of military personnel, firemen, policemen, and members of patriotic organizations. The flag represents a living country and is itself considered a living thing. Therefore, the lapel flag pin being a replica, should be worn on the left lapel near the heart.

(k) The flag, when it is in such condition that it is no longer a fitting emblem for display, should be destroyed in a dignified way, preferably by burning.

Other flag traditions include:

When flown from a pole, the fly end of the flag should be able to move freely. It should not be secured to a frame.

Display the flag only during dayling during good weather. Take it down when it gets dark or if it begins to rain or snow. It may be flown at night in good weather if it is lighted.

The flag should not be draped on a car or podium (instead use red, white, and blue bunting with the blue on top).

When the flag is used to cover a casket, the canton (star area) should be placed over the left shoulder. The flag should be removed before the casket is lowered into the grave.

When displayed on the wall, the flag's canton should be on the left as you view it.

On U.S. Army uniforms the flag patch is usually worn on the right shoulder. It looks back to front as seen in a mirror. That is to give the effect of the flag flying behind in the breeze as the wearer moves forward.

To store the flag, fold it in half twice, width-wise. Then fold up a triangle, starting at the striped end and repeat until only the end of the union is exposed. Then fold down the square into a triangle and tuck it inside the folds.

Oaths & Pledges

NATURALIZATION OATH

I hereby declare, on oath, that I absolutely and entirely renounce and abjure all allegiance and fidelity to any foreign prince, potentate, state, or sovereignty of whom or which I have heretofore been a subject or citizen; that I will support and defend the Constitution and laws of the United States of America against all enemies, foreign and domestic; that I will bear true faith and allegiance to the same; that I will bear arms on behalf of the United States when required by the law; that I will perform noncombatant service in the Armed Forces of the United States when required by the law; that I will perform work of national importance under civilian direction when required by the law; and that I take this obligation freely without any mental reservation or purpose of evasion; so help me God.

PLEDGE OF ALLEGIANCE

"I pledge allegiance to the Flag
of the United States of America
and to the Republic for which it stands,
one nation [under God], indivisible,
with liberty and justice for all."

The original Pledge of Allegiance was written in 1892 by Francis Bellamy, a Baptist minister and prominent Boston socialist. It was first recited by schoolchildren on Columbus Day that year—the 400th anniversary of the explorer's discovery of America. Its recitation soon became a daily ritual in public schools, though it was not given any official government sanction until 1942 in the United States Flag Code. The Supreme Court held in 1943 that children could not be forced to take part in the daily pledge ritual. The wording has been modified three times, most significantly with the controversial addition of the phrase "under God" in 1954.

SELECTED US FLAGS 1777–TODAY

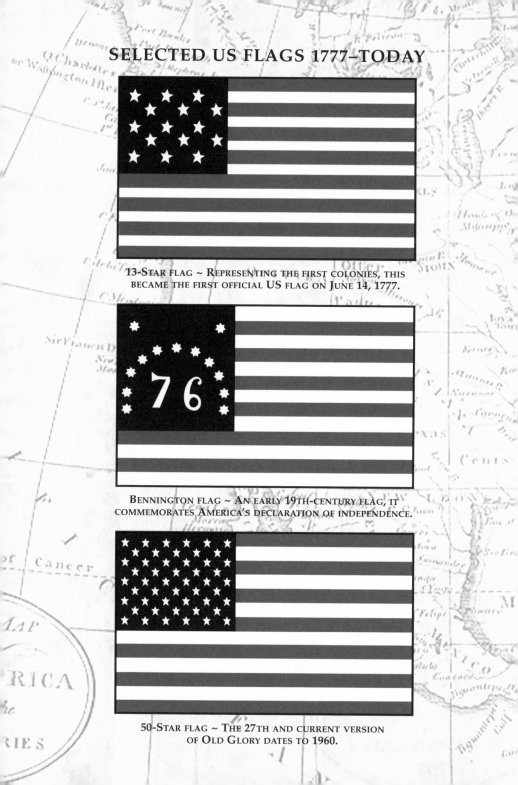

13-STAR FLAG ~ REPRESENTING THE FIRST COLONIES, THIS BECAME THE FIRST OFFICIAL US FLAG ON JUNE 14, 1777.

BENNINGTON FLAG ~ AN EARLY 19TH-CENTURY FLAG, IT COMMEMORATES AMERICA'S DECLARATION OF INDEPENDENCE.

50-STAR FLAG ~ THE 27TH AND CURRENT VERSION OF OLD GLORY DATES TO 1960.